Workers' Education

A.B.S.V. Ranga Rao

ABHIJEET PUBLICATIONS
DELHI 110 094

ABHIJEET PUBLICATIONS
2/46 Tukhmeerpur Extension
Delhi 110094
Phones: 011-22960492, 65698474
e-mail: abhijeetpublication@gmail.com
abhijeet_singh1@indiatimes.com

WORKERS' EDUCATION

First Published 2008

ISBN 978-81-89886-37-0

Price: Rs. 620/- (INR)

PRINTED IN INDIA

Published by J.K. Singh fo Abhijeet Publications, Delhi 110094, Lasertypeset by Gaurav Graphics, Delhi and Printed as Himanshu Printers, Delhi.

Acknowledgements

I express my profound thanks to Prof. B.S. Murthy, Department of Industrial Relations and Personnel Management, Andhra University for providing me with invaluable and scholarly guidance in bringing out this work.

I place on record my gratitude to my teacher and mentor, Prof. B.R.K. Raju, Department of Social Work, Andhra University whose attention and eagerness enabled my work on workers education reach its logical conclusion.

I deem it appropriate to thank Dr. D.K. Lal Das, Principal, College of Social Work, Hyderabad and Dr. M.S.S. Kama Raju for offering their precious suggestions during my study.

My thanks are also due to my friend and colleague Dr. S.V. Sudhakar for his continuous support in my endeavour and my friend Dr. K. Sekhar who has also helped me considerably. I owe a lot to them.

My precious thanks are due to my teachers and colleagues, Prof. B. Vijaya Lakshmi, Prof. B. Devi Prasad, Dr. N. Babayya, Dr. K. Visveswara Rao, Dr. R.D. Sampath Kumar, Dr. T. Sobhasri, Dr. P. Arjun, Dr. C. Bapu Haranath who were of perennial sources of encouragement and inspiration to me.

My thanks are also due to Sri J. Prasad, P. Satyanarayana and Ms. K. Swarna Kumari who helped me in the collection of data. I also record my sincere thanks to Ms. K. Vijaya Lakshmi, and Sri Rayudu of Central Board of Workers' Education whose assistance provided quite useful to me in gathering information pertaining to my research. Sincerely, I owe a great deal to my respondents for their cooperation in giving information and sharing their experiences with me. My deepest thanks go to Mr. D.V. Jagannadha Rao who typed the manuscript and helped me in giving final shape to the work.

I also place on record my deep sense of gratitude to Dr. A.D. Mishra, Deputy Director, National Gandhi Museum, New Delhi for his unstinted support and encouragement throughout the study.

I am also thankful to M/s Abhijeet Publications whose efforts helped me in translating the research work into book form.

Finally it is my bounden duty to express my deep sense of gratitude to my family members particularly my father, whose affection kept my spirits alive and whose blessings saw the work through.

A.B.S.V. RANGA RAO

Preface

A tripartite semi-autonomous body known as the Central Board for Workers' Education was set up in 1958 under the Ministry of Labor, Govt. of India to formulate policies and programmes and to administer a three-tier Workers' Education Scheme. The objectives enunciated in the programme include strengthening the trade union movement by imparting knowledge that will make the workers have a greater understandings of the problems of social and economic environment; for their intelligent participation in accordance with the declared objectives of the state and to develop leadership among the workers and to make the trade unions run on democratic lines.

For achieving its objective the board has developed a need based, three-tier training programme. In the first phase, training will be given to the educational officers who will be posted in different regional centers across the country. The regional centers conduct the worker-teacher training programme to selected workers of the industries situated in their jurisdiction. The workers after undergoing training in the regional centers conduct classes in their units to the trainee workers.

The Workers' Education Scheme has been subjected to several critical evaluations from time to time. Review of the studies on workers education revealed the majority of the studies concentrated on workers or worker-trainees and on their perception of the impact, thus neglecting the worker-teacher on whose shoulders the responsibility of conducting unit level classes and imparting education rests. The progress, whatsoever, made by the board in the field of workers education is the result of efforts of the worker-teachers.

It is against this background that the present study of Workers' education is taken up to the study the perceptions of the worker-teachers towards the effectiveness of the Workers' education scheme by eliciting their opinions/views on various aspects of the scheme. Visakhapatnam Regional Center was selected for the study as it the second largest city in the State of Andhra Pradesh and nerve center of all industrial activities of coastal Andhra Pradesh.

There are limited publications on the subject of workers education. The latest book on workers education was published in mid-eighties. The present study on workers education throw light on different aspects of the present scheme and it will be useful to the policy planners, Labour Educators and students of labour welfare.

THE AUTHOR

Contents

1

Introduction

What is Education

The social structure of any society is composed of social groups and institutions established and sustained from time to time. The sustenance is the result of transmission of values and beliefs to the younger generations who replace the older generations. The knowledge imparted to the young enables them to contribute to the survival of the society. The young must be preserved physically and initiated socially if the life of the society or group is to continue. As biological life maintains and transmits itself by mutation and reproduction, social life sustains itself by education. The means whereby a social group continues itself, maintains its ideals is in the broadest sense of the term Education (Horne, 1932)[1]. Anderson (1972)[2] viewed education "as the process of communicating of knowledge and shaping of values and in that sense, it is synonymous with socialisation. Imparting of knowledge is the basic thing for the survival of the society. Stressing the same point, Ross (1942)[3] observed, "Society's primary and foremost occupation is education". To Durkheim (1956)[4] "Education is the influence exercised by adult generations on those that are not yet ready for social life. Its object is to arouse and develop in the child a certain number of physical, intellectual and moral states, which are demanded of him by both the political society as a whole and the social milieu for which he is specially destined. In a wider perspective education is a socialisation process through which a person learns the vocation of his or her life. In almost all societies education is the vehicle for transmission of culture, skills, values and belief systems and prepares an individual for working life (Dewey 1944).

Education is the process of helping people to develop their minds and become intelligent members of the social order. "Its aim is not man power but manhood (Hutchins 1968)[6]. Its aim is to dovetail the culture of the country in which it is imparted. Education should also acquaint us with our ignorance. Socrates (1963)[7] the greatest Philosopher and thinker once commented "I know nothing except the fact of my ignorance". Education apart from enlightening the people and helping them to know their ignorance, acts as a guide in helping them eradicate social ills.

In addition to imparting knowledge education also teaches behaviour. Ruskin (1951)[8] once remarked—Education does not mean teaching people what they do not know; it means teaching them to behave as they do not behave. To Whitehead (1929)[9] education is the acquisition of the art of the utilisation of the knowledge. Dewey[10] conceived education as having its implications, in social, moral economic and political spheres. Theories of democracy hold that education is a correlate of democratic order. Hasley and others (1961)[11] have shown concern for the determinants of educational system in the other sectors of society.

It has been universally recognised that the strength of democracy depends upon the character and intelligence of all its citizens. As Dewey (1944)[12] puts it "the devotion of democracy to education is a familiar fact". A government resting on popular suffrage cannot be successful unless those who elect and obey their governors are educated. Democracy offers immense freedom for the individual. It is the only education that helps him interpret freedom in terms of responsibility. It is only a means for the widespread diffusion of democratic ideals. To Plato (1933)[13] "education is the basis of state ... and the ultimate aim and essence of education is the training of character".

Economists also recognised the importance of education. Alfred Marshall (1961)[14] emphasised the importance of education "as a material investment" and in his view education is "the most valuable of all capital is that invested in human being." He stressed the role of skills in increasing production and specifically identified education of workers not only as a target but also an instrument of economic development. The idea of investment in Man, for developing human resources, is gaining ground in the developing countries. To assess the investment in Man in terms of the yield of physical resources and increase in productivity is not a proper view. But in terms of improved human capacity, better management of human affairs in public or private affairs and the general well-being of people, Education has its yield in qualitative aspect (Lewis, Arthur, W., 1962)[15].

Apart from political and social imperatives, the realization that education is indispensable had led almost all the countries to adopt universal and free education as their primary goal and embarked on educating their citizens.

A great drawback in developing countries like ours is the presence of a large mass of illiterate and semi-literate compared to better educated. The remarks of T.H. Huxley (1901)[16] is worth mentioning.

"The politicians tell us 'you must educate the masses because they are going to be masters'. The clergy join the cry for education for they affirm that the people are drifting away from church and chapel into the broadest infidelity. The manufacturers and the capitalists swell the chorus lustily. They declare that ignorance makes bad workmen 'that England will soon be unable to turn out cotton goods, or steam engines, cheaper than other people; and then, the glory will be departed from us. And a few voices are lifted up in favour of the doctrine that the masses should be educated because they are men and women with unlimited capacity of being, doing and suffering, and that it is as true now, as ever it was that the people perish for lack of knowledge".

Bodete (1951)[17] observed: "as peace is indivisible so are democracy and social progress indivisible. As long as half of the human race is unable to read the very declaration of its duties and rights to understand the text of the law, to consult the most elementary books on agriculture and machinery, it will continue to be at the mercy of forces which it can neither control nor comprehend. And we have to admit that democracy does not reign on earth".

Thomas Jefferson wrote in 1820[18] "I know no safe depositors of ultimate power of society, but the people themselves and if we think they are not enlightened enough to exercise their discretion, the remedy is not to take it from them, but to inform their discretion by education".

While the early years of life are important for mental development, it is equally true that human being is capable of learning through out life. The education of the masses who are deprived of formal schooling comes under the broad field of adult education. The term adult education is also designated as life long learning, continuous learning, extension education, night schools, etc.

Adult Education

Adult Education, according to Verner (1962)[19] is the action of an external education agent in purposefully ordering behaviour into planned systematic experiences that can result in learning for those for whom such activity is supplemented to their primary role in society, and which involved some continuity in an exchange relationship between the agent and the learner so that the educational process is under constant supervision and direction". Education has assumed different forms in various cultural settings, the method of Adult Education is culture specific. In view of this the methods adopted in one culture cannot be transferred to dissimilar cultures. Therefore, adult education assumes different forms in different places and periods. The British society made pioneering effort in the spread of adult education in different forms in western society. The nineteenth century cultural settings gave rise to the folk schools in Denmark while Adult Education Schools flourished in Scandinavian countries, England and the United States. Several distinctive methods of Adult Education have originated in the U.S. Peffer (1926)[20] spoke of the open forum, university extension, correspondence schools and various educational agencies for youth. According to him "Adult education is taken, as education outside the usual formal channels for men and women engaged in the ordinary pursuits of life; or, simpler as the efforts of grown persons to go on learning while earning a living".

Some Perspectives on Adult Education

Maygood and Leveright (1968) defined adult education as "process whereby persons, who no longer (did not) attend school on a formal, regular and full time basis undertake sequential and organised activities with a conscious intention of bringing about changes in information, knowledge, understanding or skills, appreciation and attitudes or for the purpose of identifying and solving personal or community problems" Mohisini (1973)[21] held that "Adult Education—tries to develop in individual adult, inherent abilities and talents necessary for the fulfillment of his personality and for his being of service to the community. Berteisen (1975)[22] contended: "Adult education embraces all forms of educative experience needed by men and women according to their varying interests and requirements at their differing levels of comprehension and ability and in their changing roles and responsibilities throughout life, irrespective of content, level and methods used".

However, there is a felt need for special educational programmes, in view of the increasing rate of economic development, the changes in labour force, the emergence of trade unions and other phenomena of social and technological change. The above factors demand from the worker an increased capacity to meet the challenge of new opportunities, to participate actively in economic and social life and to deal effectively with the problems confronting him and his fellow workers.

The need for coping with the changed circumstances and socio-economic development, and developing the one's awareness about her/his predicament in the cultural milieu has necessitated the emergence of a new form of education to meet the needs of the workers as it was felt the prevalent adult education programmes were too broad based to cater to the specific needs of the workers.

Workers Education

As in case of other progressive movements, the impetus for extending education to workers came from England. In the backdrop of the industrial revolution and the resultant rise of social problems, education was seen as one of the remedies for combating social decay. The workers' education programme is an attempt to neutralize the dehumanizing effects of factory labour. It consisted of programmes aimed at offering working people with a quality of liberal arts education outside of school system which excluded them (Harriet Katz: 1978)[23].

The seminal ideas on workers education can be found in Peffer's (1924)[24] work. According to him the workers in their desire to progress themselves as a class "desire self-improvement, of course, like other adults who give part of their leisure to learning; but they desire it as members of a class with a special interest, in the belief that by educating themselves they will be better able to advance their collective interest, to modify, if not to remould their social order at least to understand it. Workers' education is adult education arising out of a social impulse and having a social purpose. Such an education is aimed to produce concrete results in training the worker in labour leadership. Walter Vrooman[25] in his opening address of Ruskin College for Workers' education in 1899 envisaged: "We shall take men who have been merely condemning our institutions and will teach them how, instead, to transform those institutions so that in place of talking against the world, they will begin methodically and scientifically to possess the world, to refashion it, and to cooperate with the power behind evolution in making it the Joyous abode of, if not a perfected humanity, at least a humanity earnestly, and rationally striving toward perfection".

Albert Mansbridge[26] who founded the workers' educational association in 1903, said "Our Association has especially sought to bring together university students, who are rich in the education afforded by books and working men, who are rich in the education afforded by life".

The Workers' Education Association believes in the

education of workers for its own sake. It is an enrichment experience, of cultural values and training in citizenship, it does not commit itself at all as to the class conflict. Livingstone (1951)[27] has made some complimentary comments "the Workers' Education Association class type, which provides both an expert and a discussion and an atmosphere as impartial as ordinary human nature allows. The workers education association was termed as a seed bed of socialism and also accused of betraying the interests of the workers by supporting capitalism. Its refusal to be partisan is more striking because it was primarily a working class movement and the views of its members were as naturally 'left' as those of well-to-do are naturally 'right', its service to political democracy in England cannot be over estimated. Its great weakness is one which it is in no way responsible; it only touches an intellectual elite".

In the context of American experience in early twentieth century, workers' education was viewed as an informal discussion group of social science subjects like, economics, psychology, history or political science, which features in the interaction between the instructor and the workmen and women, regarding their needs and also drawing out their experiences relating to the subject and interpret the subject in terms of those experiences in the subjects (Peffer, 1920)[28].

Viewing workers education as a special type of adult education the American educationist Edward Lindman (1984)[29] predicted that all successful adult education groups some day will become social action groups. He praised Grundtvig for doing pioneering work by establishing Danish Folk High Schools and organising the British workers education movements.

According to Harry Laidler (1973)[30] workers' education is an attempt on the part of the organised labour to educate its own members within the framework of an educational system in which the workers prescribe the courses of instruction, select the teachers and also finance the exercise. He stated that workers education is a charge upon the trade unions to educate its own members. He further called for such an educational system in which the workers themselves prepare the curricula and syllabi and select the teachers and which has to be financed out of the resources of the concerned unions.

Shukla (1971)[31] went further and said that the educational activity should also take place in a trade union setting. In his words "workers' education aims at social action and such action is the result of the educational process that takes place within the same setting of a trade union, rather than in any other group got together merely for educational purpose. Workers education in contrast to other types of adult education seeks to help the worker to solve her/his problems not as an individual, but as member of her/his class (Perlman, S. 1932)[32]. According to Florence Peterson (1951)[33] "Workers' Education, as commonly used, is not a general term but has a specific connotation. It is a specific kind of adult education, designed to provide the workers, with better understanding of their rights, status and responsibilities as workers' union members, consumers and citizens. Workers' education emphasizes group advancement and solution of group problems and thus differs from vocational and professional education which is primarily training for individual advancement. The definition of Florence Peterson to some extent not only clarified the difference between workers' education and other educational programmes but also sought to draw our attention to the difference between adult education and workers' education. The salient features of workers' education according to her are *(a)* it is a special kind of adult education meant for workers, and *(b)* it lays stress on group advancement, while other educational programmes aim at individual advancement.

In view of the rapidly changing scope of workers' education, many of the definitions of workers education by the practitioners based on the particular needs of the target groups, may not be applicable to workers' education in general (C. Fernau: 1984)[34]. In his analysis "Workers' Education is carried out by trade unions, rural workers' organisation and workers educational institutions or by specialist institutions such as Universities, in collaboration with workers' organisation... Workers education is intended to meet the educational needs of workers, and their organisations in the defence of their acquired rights and the satisfaction of their individual, social, economic and cultural aspirations". Such an education is future oriented.

Workers' education is not pointed education, *i.e.* education aimed to produce concrete results and confined to that aim. It is pointed education in so far as it trains men in the technique of labour leadership, but that constitutes only a small part (Peffer: 1926)[35]. It need not be, however, and for the greater part a propagandist education. There is, it is true, a faction in organised labour which holds that workers' education is valueless unless it is systemised educational propaganda directed against the employing class, if not against capitalism as an institution.

Workers' education is thus designed basically to enhance the workers' understanding of labour problems. It is not an end in itself and should always be regarded as a means to useful action. It has been said that the end of education is to be found in the individual's growth in power to cope with his environment. Almost all national, regional and international trade union movements have committed themselves to educating their members to take up economic and social responsibilities.

Workers' Education: Different Approaches

The scope of the workers education, according to Robinson (1966)[36], is to train the workers, to become trade union members and participate in collective bargaining. He added that workers' education's aim was to narrow the gap between the workers with formal education and other groups and to enable the workers to play a creative role in all civic affairs as individuals and representatives of their trade unions.

The approaches to workers' education range from purely practical educational needs of workers and trade unions to highly idealistic objective of creating "society based on social and economic justice". The wide ranging variations in approaches to workers' education may be in accordance with the varied social, economic and cultural conditions or needs of the nations in which the programmes are organised. A major view point is that the workers' education should be confined to the creation of awareness about their rights and responsibilities as workers. This school essentially takes a functional view of the role of education vis-a-vis the needs of industrial enterprises and trade unions.

A slightly modified and broader approach is that the workers' education should try to create consciousness among workers about their role as union members. The International Confederation of Free Trade Unions (ICFTU) (1956)[37] observed that the "chief aim of workers' education is to train the members of trade unions to take more active interest in the trade union movement. According to V.S. Mathur (1964)[38] workers' education is expected to encourage the workers to take active part in their respective organisations and to discharge effectively their responsibility towards the trade union movement and the community in general".

The very objective of creating trade union consciousness among workers has brought to fore the concept of trade union education. Workers' education and trade union education are used interchangeably and the difference between the two is negligible. But there is some difference in the scope of the terms. Workers' education is wider term compared to trade union education. Trade union education confines itself to training workers in trade unionism and to become active trade union members, whereas workers' education, besides training the workers in trade unionism aims at imparting social and basic education. It seeks to make a worker not only a good trade unionist, but also a responsible citizen, enhance his utility to his employer as well as to the society.

According to the report of the international seminar at Brussels (ICFTU, 1958)[39] the term trade union education should be applied only to educational work conducted by or under the auspices of trade unions, with participants who are members of trade unions. The programme should be directly related to the aims and activities of trade unions with a specific purpose of enabling workers to acquire the knowledge, techniques and militant free trade union spirit essential for their active participation in the work of movement".

Another school maintains that the purpose of workers

education is to create consciousness among workers about their rights and duties not only as workers, but members of the trade union and citizens. Jack Barbash (1955)[40] for instance defined workers' education as any planned educational activity which a union undertakes or any educational activity undertaken by any agency other than union, whose major objective is to build more effective union and citizenship. This emphasis on citizenship education, therefore, adds a new dimension to the workers' education. It wants workers to be trained in trade union matters not merely as union members, but by keeping in view the larger perspective of their duties and responsibilities as citizens. As pointed out by International Labour Organisation[41] workers education has to take into account the educational needs of the worker as an individual for his personal evolution; as an operative—for his efficiency and advancement; as a citizen—for a happy and integrated life in the community; as member of a trade union—for the protection of his interests as a member of the working class. This view of workers' education underscores the primacy of social and national interests over sectional interests of workers.

Another perspective argues that the objective of the workers' education should be to train and prepare the workers for participative management. It should be confined to inculcating in workers, attitudes and values conducive to the promotion of industrial democracy. Robinson (1966)[42] felt that the broad concept of workers education should focus on the narrower concept of education which seeks to equip workers as trade union members and officers to carryout intelligently the collective bargaining functions. According to Ramaswamy (1985)[43] the basic concern of workers' education is not education *per se* but education that will prepare workers for participative management.

In some countries where there is dearth of leaders among the rank and file and where outsiders dominate the trade union movement, workers' education takes the form of leadership training course. Elaborating the point Cohan (1943)[44] listed three important functions of education.

1. Discovering promising young people with ability to

lead and training them in their unions or in colleges, enabling them to serve their unions in various ways.
2. Training the rank and file for assuming better positions in the democratic process within the unions and in
3. Inspiring workers towards ideologies during preparations and execution of the programme.

Thus the concept of workers' education shows a broad assortment of values which range from purely serving the needs of trade unions at one end to promoting the total development of individual worker at the other. Each one of this school views different aspects of workers' education with different emphases. Labour education is as broad as life itself and as narrow as immediate needs of the union which conducts the education. It is thus capable of being defined in a number of ways, and irrespective of the definition, labour education is always purposive in nature and oriented to solve the problems of the unions, its members and the labour movement of which it is a part. It represents the workers own instrument to make themselves more effective and their lives more satisfied.

Since the workers education programmes tend to differ from country to country in accordance with social economic and cultural factors, no common line can be drawn for all countries. The workers' education should also include adult education as it shares the basic objective of helping an individual to increase his understanding and develop his ability for creative thinking; social and economic education, as it includes all educational activities concerning the structure of human society and the relations of man to man in social and economic processes; cultural education; cultural studies and educational aspects of recreational activities; literacy and primary education where the workers are illiterate; technical and vocational education for getting more skilled and trained workers; and fundamental education so as to help people in the less developed areas to understand the problems of their environment to acquire a body of knowledge and skill for the progressive improvement of their living conditions and to participate more effectively in the economic and social development of their community (UNESCO: 1952)[45].

Workers' Education: Indian Context

The concept of workers' education is not new to India. It was there as far back as in 1920s during the British rule. The importance of workers' education was realized by the Royal Commission on Labour (1931)[46], which stated "in India nearly the whole of industrial labour is illiterate—state of affairs which is unknown in any other country of industrial importance.... Modern machine industry depends in a peculiar degree on education and the attempt to build it up with an illiterate body of workers must be deficient and perlious. We should emphasize the fact that precisely because of this, the education of industrial labour should receive special attention.

The Indian industrial landscape has changed significantly after the advent of independence. Starting from agro-based industries, the accent was shifted to capital intensive heavy industries. The rapid industrialisation and the resultant urbanisation process have trigged migration of people from rural to urban areas in search of opportunities. This has spawned different categories of workers, ranging from unorganised peasant casual workers to highly organised industrial workers. Given the level of socio-cultural matrix from which the workers had emerged and moved on to the industrial scene, they had to face adaptive problems which led to tensions at various levels. The long Indian experience with planning and industrial development, has been fraught with problems (workers). The various labour policies formulated and legislations enacted from time to time reflect the attempts made to solve such problems. However, the problems India faced, in the process, led to the realisation, that for quicker attainment of industrial democracy one has to make an attempt at inculcating the prerequisite norms for industrial democracy through workers' education scheme.

Economic development requires harnessing of all human resources of the country to achieve the desired results. Along with capital, the skills and knowledge of workers led to economic development. Hence, the need for workers' education. The need for workers' education in India was equally felt by the trade unions, employers and government. In the trade union movement one of the first to emphasise the need of education for the workers was Mahatma Gandhi. He attached importance to education of workers so that they might know their rights and obligations. He emphasized that trade union leaders should themselves be trained first. Accordingly the Hind Mazdoor Sabha[47] in its Manifesto adopted in 1948 declared "the conception of modern trade union demands that the workers must adequately be equipped with sufficient education to man the trade union offices to grapple with the problem of national importance—economic as well as political. Workers' education capable of fulfilling this task must receive top priority from free trade union movement".

Divensen, (1960)[48] the then president of Hind Mazdoor Sabha, felt that "the importance of workers' education in the present phase of trade union movement can hardly be minimised. In spite of various weakness, the trade union movement in India, has passed into a new phase calling for a different quality of leadership". The All-India Trade Union Congress in 1952[49] pointed out that "in order to develop the strength of class solidarity of the working class in defence of its interests, it is necessary that workers, are helped to overcome the lack of economic and political education on the basis of common world" (1960). The Indian National Trade Union Congress[50] in its report of the 12th session, stressed the need for workers' education and remarked that "worker is the central figure of the entire activities of a trade union. If the movement has to be strengthened, it is necessary that there is a well-planned programme for education of worker to enable him to know his status, rights and responsibilities to the members of his family and to the entire society".

The concept of workers' education its scope, contents, methods and techniques have been the theme of some of the national and international seminars held in India during the period 1954-1963. It was concluded that in India the term workers' education should cover all employees eligible for membership of trade unions as well as artisans and other self-employed persons belonging to the same social class. It also stressed the inclusion of general liberal education, vocational education and trade union education into workers' education. The participants of these seminars were of the view that the methods must allow greatest amount of participation of beneficiaries in the educational process.

The Second Five-Year Plan (1956)[51] categorically recommended increased association of labour in building a progressive state and further stated "for the achievement of industrial democracy strong trade union movement is necessary. Of course, multiplicity of trade unions which is a general problem everywhere is hampering the growth of healthy trade unionism in India. Widespread prevalence of ignorance and literacy among the workers further led to the domination of outsiders in unions, as a result, political rivalries crept into the trade union movement; then small size and the unsound financial position and inter and intra union rivalries were hampering the growth of trade unionism in India.

Keeping these focal points in view the second five year plan recognised that for the achievement of industrial democracy, strong trade union movement, improvement in the trade union finances, rendering them representative character and promotion of leadership from rank and file are essential. Training of workers in trade union philosophy and methods becomes necessary for the workers to discover leaders from within.

The successive five year plans also recognized that for the success of industrialisation on which the country has embarked, attention towards improving the quality of workforce is needed. One of the important means for securing better quality of labour is by pursuing programmes which are broadly covered under the label "workers' education".

Workers Education Scheme in India

A tripartite semi-autonomous body known as the Central Board for Workers' Education, was set up in 1958 under the Ministry of Labour, Govt. of India to formulate policies and programmes and to administer a three tier Workers' Education Scheme.

Aims and Objectives of the Scheme

The aims and objectives of the Workers' Education Scheme are:—

(i) to strengthen among all sections of the working class including workers, a sense of patriotism, national integrity, unity, amity, communal harmony, secularism and pride in being an Indian.

(ii) to equip all sections of workers including rural workers for their intelligent participation in social and economic development of the nation in accordance with its declared objectives;

(iii) to develop among workers a greater understanding of the problems of their social and economic environment, their responsibilities towards family members and their rights and obligations, as citizens, as workers, in industry, and members and officials of their trade unions;

(iv) to develop leadership from among the rank and file of workers themselves;

(v) to develop strong, united and more responsible trade unions through more enlightened members and better trained officials;

(vi) to strengthen democratic processes and traditions in the trade union movement; and

(vii) to enable trade unions themselves to take over the functions of workers' education, ultimately.

For achieving its objectives the board has developed a need-based, three-tier training programme.

First Stage

The first phase in the execution of the scheme is the training of teacher—administrators or education officers. They are selected by the board through open competition and are given training for six months by the staff of the board. The officers in turn, after the successful completion of their training course, are posted to Regional Centres.

Second Stage

The second stage and the most important phase of workers' education programme is the training of worker-teachers who are responsible for imparting education to the rank and file of workers at the unit level in the third stage. The education officers on completion of their training are posted to different regional centres. They are entrusted with the training of prospective teachers from among the workers in a full time training course of three months duration. These selected workers are known as worker-teachers'. The training of worker-teacher is a continuous process at each Regional Centre, which is expected, to train 70-100 worker-teachers in a year.

Third Stage

The worker-teachers, on completion of training at regional centres, revert to their respective establishments and conduct classes for the rank and file workers at unit level mostly, during non-working hours.

The duration of the training at unit level is usually of three months and managements provide accommodation, furniture and 45 minutes time-off to workers for attending the classes. In case of existence of all facilities, full time unit level classes of three weeks duration are also organised. After completion of their training the workers are taken to a tour of industrial centres in the country to familiarise themselves with the other industrial centres and to enable them to exchange their experiences with the workers at other centres.

Syllabus

The syllabus course content for the programme include 'know your country', 'productivity', trade unions movement, industrial relations, workers' participation in management, public sector and its role in the economy, labour economics, population education and labour legislation. The regional centre is the focal point of the activities covering the training of worker-teachers and supervision of unit level classes.

The syllabus for the three tier structure of training had been formulated since its inception was modified from time to time based on the recommendations of various committees. The present syllabus which has been presented in the following pages has been the result of the recommendations of the Syllabus Review Committee (1982).

Syllabus for Education Officers

The training programe of the Education Officers is of six months' duration, five months are meant for teaching and one month for practical training by way of attachment with the trade union organisations, Employers and Government Labour Departments.

Table 1.1
Syllabus for Education Officers

S.No.	*Contents*	*Modules*	*Sessions*
1.	Introduction	6	20
2.	Know your country	8	32
3.	Know your industry	6	21
4.	Productivity Education	6	22
5.	Industrial Relations	5	20
6.	Trade Union Movement	15	40
7.	Labour Economics	6	22
8.	Education for Participative Management	4	15
9.	Public Sector and Its Role in Economy	5	18
10.	Population Education and Family Welfare	6	34
11.	Important Labour Legislations	3	40
12.	Methods, Tools and Techniques of Communication and Practicals	10	196
		80	480

The syllabus for the training of educational officers has

been developed on modular basis, with modules having different units depending upon the scope and importance of the topics. Normally, 120 working days are available out of five months teaching period. Thus at the rate of 4 sessions per day 90 minutes each, 480 sessions are allotted for covering the syllabus.

Table 1.2

Syllabus and Time Allotted for Worker-Teacher Training

S.No.	*Contents*	*Modules*	*Study Units*	*Percentage*
1.	Introduction	10	13	5.2
2.	Know your country	7	20	8.0
3.	Know your industry	7	8	3.2
4.	Productivity Education	5	15	6.0
5.	Industrial Relations	6	11	4.4
6.	Trade Union Movement	13	21	8.4
7.	Labour Economics	7	16	6.4
8.	Education for Participative Management	5	10	4.0
9.	Public Sector and Its Role in Economy	5	11	4.4
10.	Population Education and Family Welfare	5	13	5.2
11.	Important Labour Legislations	3	21	8.4
12.	Methods, Tools and Techniques of Communication and Practicals	14	91	36.4
	Total	87	250	100.0

Syllabus for Worker-Teachers

The syllabus drawn for the worker-teacher is not different from the one designed for education officer. There is similarity in syllabus for both Education Officers and worker-teachers. It is only with regard to details, variation can be envisaged taking into account the capacity of the education officers to impart what has been imbibed and the level of understanding of the prospective worker-teachers. The worker-teacher training course is of 13 weeks duration. Topics pertaining to local needs of industry and workers employed therein can be covered with the approval of the Regional Advisory Committee. Flexibility is allowed to the Education Officers at the Regional Centre to re-arrange the syllabus depending on the composition of the worker-teacher trainees.

The communication techniques—practicals, which have been allotted 91 hours in the syllabus are divided into 14 modules or sections.

Section-1	:	The nature of learning process How mature adults learn communication methods 3 hours
Section-2	:	Methods of persuasion Active teaching techniques for literate and illiterate rural labour workers—preparation for teaching and use of library 1 hour
Section-3	:	Leading/moderating group discussions, seminar, symposia, panel discussions, debate and role play 5 hours
Section-4	:	Importance of using visual aids in teaching 1 hour
Section-5	:	Use of flip charts, flash cards, flannel graphs, posters, films, film-strips, slides and epidia scope 2 hours
Section-6	:	Role and responsibility of worker-teachers 1 hour
Section-7	:	Organising unit level class 1 hour
Section-8	:	Literature for workers-reports and information regarding unit level classes to be submitted to Regional Centres 1 hour
Section-9	:	Planning of an industrial tour or local excursion 2 hours
Section-10	:	Motivation-different means and methods 2 hours
Section-11	:	Importance of non-formal adult education-teaching and learning by adults 1 hour
		20 hours

Section-12 :	Practicals in use of audio-visual aids	
(a) Use of black board		5 hours
(b) Use of flash cards, flannel graphs and poster		5 hours
(c) Use of flip charts, bar graphs		5 hours
(d) Use of films, film-strips, slides, etc.		5 hours
Section-13 :	Practice teaching	17 hours
		37 hours
Section-14 :	Field visits and report writing	
(a) Union meeting		5 hours
(b) Conciliation proceedings		5 hours
(c) Hearing in a labour court		5 hours
(d) Union movement negotiations		5 hours
(e) Working of a State Labour Dept.		5 hours
Periodic tests and examinations		10 hours
		35 hours

Elementary Yoga/Physical exercises should be organised for 15 minutes every day before commencing the programme.

Syllabus for Unit Level Classes (ULC)

The scheme did not prescribe any syllabus separately for the unit level classes and the syllabus of worker-teacher training course is followed for the unit level classes. The local committee has the freedom to develop separate programme taking into consideration the needs of the situations and capacity of the worker-teachers.

Refresher Course

Refresher courses are also conducted to worker-teachers to regain what they have lost in past months. The worker-teachers who are engaged at units are imparted further training by way of refresher courses of about a week duration.

Every worker-teacher who is engaged in conducting classes at the unit level is paid Rs. 100/- as honorarium for the additional work which he puts in organising the classes. The worker-teacher has to stay in the premises of the factory for one and half hour after the normal working hours as the classes are held out side the working hours.

Study Tours

Study tour is undertaken for the trainees at the unit level so that the outlook of the workers may be widened and that they may familiarise themselves with the conditions prevailing in different establishments.

There are no hard and fast rules for selecting the workers for unit level classes. It is the job of the worker-teacher to select the workers. Since the worker-teacher conducts classes in the unit, and he might be knowing the workers, the job of selecting them is left to him.

Apart from the above programme for the organised sector specified in the preceding pages, the Central Board for Workers' Education conducts various training programmes for the unorganised/small scale, rural and informal sector workers.

National level programmes are conducted by the Indian Institute of Workers Education while regional and unit level programmes are conducted through a network of 48 regional, 15 sub-regional centers spread throughout the country. The four zonal Directors established by the Board of Delhi, Mumbai, Kolkata and Chennai supervise and monitor the activities of the Regional Centres under their respective zones.

Grants-in-Aid

The board assists or extends financial assistance to trade unions for conducting their own workers education programme through its grants-in-aid scheme introduced in 1960. Funds are provided in the Board's budget for giving grants-in-aid to the registered trade unions and other institutions whose membership is not based on race, caste and religion for conducting their own workers education programme.

One of the objectives of the board is to encourage central trade unions to set up departments of workers education and smaller unions to conduct workers education programme on a continuing basis with the board's grants-in-aid assistance.

Progress

The Central Board for Workers Education through its network of 48 regional, 15 sub-regional centres spread throughout the country implements and conducts educational programmes to the workers in the organised, unorganised and rural sectors. Since its inception in 1958, it has trained 735 education officers, 86,780 worker-teachers and 4,011,866 workers in the unit level classes till March 2000.

Statement of the Problem

The central board of workers education which was entrusted with the task of implementing workers education programme to the workers of organised, un-organised and rural workers has completed 42 years since its inception. During this 42 years of period it has trained 86,780 worker-teachers, 4,011,866 worker-trainees in the unit level classes through a network of 48 regional centres and 15 sub-regional centres spread all over the country. In the wake of its tremendous progress made in the field of workers education it was considered worthwhile to study and assess critically the scheme at the micro-level *i.e.* regional centre level. No worthwhile study on different aspects of the scheme was made in Andhra Pradesh. Hence, the present study is an attempt to examine the implementation of the programme at Visakhapatnam regional centre and this study is confined to the scheme relating to the organised sector.

References

1. Horne, H.H. (1932) *The Democratic Philosophy of Education*, McMillan, New York.
2. Anderson Arnold, C. (1972) *Education and Society*, International Encyclopaedia of Social Sciences, McMillan, New York, Vol. 31, pp. 517-525.

3. Ross, J.S. (1942) *Ground Work Educational Theory*, London: George G. Harrap & Co. Ltd., p. 17.
4. Durkheim, Emile (1956) *Education and Society*, Glencoe, III: Free Press, p. 71.
5. Dewey John (1944) *Democracy and Education*, New York: McMillan Co., p. 87.
6. Robert H.H. (1968) *The Learning Society*, Chicago, USA: Brittanica Perspectives, Chicago.
7. Socrates (1963) *The Pocket Book of Quotations*, Cardinal Edition, Henry Davidoff, New York, p. 75.
8. Ruskin (1951) *Some Tasks for Education by Richard Living Stone*, Oxford University Press, Mumbai, p. 24.
9. Whitehead, A.N. (1929) *The Aims of Education*, The Macmillan Co., New York, p. 13.
10. Dewey John (1944) *Democracy and Education*, McMillan Co., New York. p. 58.
11. Hasley *et. al.* (Ed.)(1961) *Education, Economy and Society*, Free Press, New York, p. 13.
12. Dewey John (1944) *Democracy and Education*, McMillan Co., New York, p. 87.
13. Plato (1933) *The Republic* (with an English translation by Paul Shorey), Heinemann, New York.
14. Marshall, Alfred (1961) *Principles of Economics*, London: Macmillan ELBS Co. Ltd., p. 179.
15. Lewis, Arthur W. (1962) *Education and Economic Development*, International Social Science Journal, Vol. XIV, p. 688.
16. Huxley (1901) Quoted in Cyril Bibby 'The Scientific Humanist Huxley in the Educated man (Ed.) Paul Orash Andreas, M., Kazamrias, Henry Y. Perkinson, Jolible & Sons Ltd., pp. 266-267.
17. Bodete Thomas (1951) *The Right to Education UNESCO*, UNESCO and Its Programme VII.
18. Jefferson, Thomas (1820) *Quoted in Education and Democracy* by N.V. Sukla, Concept, New Delhi, p. 10.
19. Verner Coolie (1962) *A Conceptual Scheme for the Identification and Classification Process for Adult Education*, Adult Education Association, pp. 2-3.
20. Peffer, Nathaniel (1926) *New Schools for Older Students*, MacMillan, London, p. 3.
21. Mohisini, S.R. (1973) *Adult and Community Education*, Indian Adult Education Association, New Delhi, p. 166.

22. Berteisen (1975) "Adult Education: A Position Paper", Unpublished paper submitted to UNESCO.

23. Harriet Katz (1978) *Workers Education or Education for Workers,* Social Service Review, Vol. 52, No. 2, The University of Chicago, Chicago.

24. Peffer, Nathaniel (1926) *New Schools for Older Students,* MacMillan, London, p. 203.

25. Vrooman Walter (1899) Quoted by Peffer Nathaniel in *New School for Older Students,* McMillan, p. 208.

26. Mansbridge Albert Quoted in Peffer Nathaniel Reference Book, New Schools for Older Students.

27. Livingstone Richard, *Some Tasks for Education,* Oxford University Press, London, p. 60.

28. Peffer, Nathaniel (1926) *New Schools for Older Students,* MacMillan, London, p. 232.

29. Lindman, Edward (1984) Quoted by C. Fernau in *What is Workers' Education?* An attempt at clarification, Labour Education, No. 57, pp. 3-5.

30. Harry Laidler (1973) Quoted in Kakkar, N.K. *Workers Education in India,* New Delhi: Sterling Publishers (Pvt.) Ltd., p. 5.

31. Shukla, P.D. (1971) *Life Long Education,* New Delhi: Orient Longman, p. 58.

32. Perlman, S. (1932) *Education,* Encyclopaedia of Social Sciences, Vol. XV, p. 484.

33. Petersons, Florene (1951) *American Labour Unions,* New Delhi: Sterling Publishers (P) Ltd., p. 137.

34. Fernau, C. (1984) *What is Workers' Education?* An attempt at clarification, Labour Education, No. 57, pp. 3-5.

35. Robinson, J.W. (1966) Book Review of An Historical Examination of the purposes and practices of the educational programmes of the United Automobile Workers of America, 1936-1959 by Thomas E. Linton, *Labour History,* Vol. VII.

37. International Confederation of Free Trade Unions (1956) Training the World Trade Unionists ICFTU, Brussels, p. 33.

38. Mathur, V.S. (1964) *Role of Labour Education in Developing Economy,* Bombay Labour Journal, July, Bombay, p. 48.

39. International Confederation of Free Trade Unions (1958) Education—The Key to Labour Progress, ICFTU (Report of the International Seminar) (1958) Brussels, p. 2.

40. Barbash, J. (1955) *Universities and Unions in Workers Education,* Harper & Brothers, New York, p. 3.

41. ILO (1973) Quoted in Pant S.C. in Indian Labour Problems, Chaitanya Publications, Allahabad, pp. 51-52.
42. Robinson, J.W. (1966) Book Review of An Historical Examination of the Purposes and Practices of the Educational Programmes of the United Automobile Workers of America, 1936-1959 by Thomas E. Linton, Labour History, Vol. VII.
43. Ramaswamy, E.A. (1985) *What Education do Workers Need?* Indian Journal of Adult Education, May 1985, Vol. 46, No. 5, pp. 20-33.
44. Cohan, F.M. (1943) *Workers Education in War & Peace,* New York: Workers' Education Bureau, New York.
45. UNESCO (1952) *UNESCO Seminar on Workers Education,* UNESCO, Paris, May, pp. 3-4.
46. Govt. of India (1931) *Report of the Royal Commission on Labour,* London, p. 28.
47. Hind Mazdoor Sabha (1948) *Manifesto of Hind Mazdoor Sabha,* HMS, New Delhi.
48. Divensen (1960) *Report of the Ninth Annual Convention,* Presidential Address, HMS, pp. 14-15.
49. AITUC (1952) *AITUC,* Report of the Annual Convention.
50. INTUC (1960) *Report of the 12th Session.*
51. Govt. of India (1956) *Second Five Year Plan Report,* Planning Commission, Govt. of India Publication, p. 578.
52. Govt. of India (1982) *Report of the Syllabus Review Committee on Training Programmes of Central Board for Workers Education,* Ministry of Labour, New Delhi, p. 32.

2

Review of Literature

It is observed that a lot of time, effort and money is spent on education and training of managerial cadres but playing little attention for Workers' education is a common feature of management. Such a feature seems to be present not only in the smaller industrial organisations but also in bigger industrial enterprises. The role of the trade unions in this respect is not commendable either. While they seem to show an ostensible interest in the education of workers, in practice, none of them appear to have any commitment, systematic programme and provision for education of their members. The field of Workers' education, though neglected both by the management and trade unions, has been receiving the government's attention with the creation of Central Board for Workers' Education in 1958.

Since the board which was entrusted with the task of implementing the Workers' education programme completed forty two years of its existence it is worthwhile to study and assess critically the scheme at the micro-level, *i.e.*, regional centre level. To proceed further in the direction of assessing the performance of the scheme, a review of the earlier studies made on the subject will be of immense value.

The Workers' education scheme which concerns the vital section of our society, *i.e.*, Workers, has been subjected to varying degrees of criticism—a total failure and hence a drain on the public exchequer; commendable as it has created an awareness among the workers in our country (Virmani[1], 1986).

Researchers in the field made different types of evaluations. The Central Board of Workers Education, itself conducted some studies, which it calls them as 'diagnostic studies' in some selected industries in different parts of the country. Trade Union leaders and I.L.O. experts also examined the various aspects of the programme in their evaluations.

The National Commission on Labour[2] (1969) appointed by the Government of India observed in its report "though training was not, unfortunately, of much help to trade union workers, it did make the trainees good workers and stimulated in them the awareness of trade unions". It further added that the beneficiaries of workers education have shown more interest in union activities than others who have not had education. The report suggested that the programme of workers' education should be formulated, administered and implemented by trade unions themselves. It emphasised the need for a totally new set of objectives for the Central Board for Workers' Education. The proposed objectives were as follows:

1. It should make the worker

(a) a responsible, committed and disciplined operator;

(b) understand the basic and technical aspects of the industry and the plant where he/she is employed so that he/she can take an intelligent interest in its affairs;

(c) aware of his rights and obligations;

(d) understand the organisation and functions of the union as well as develop qualities of leadership, loyality and devotion towards trade union work so that he can intelligently participate in the affairs of his unions;

(e) lead a clean and healthy life on a firm ethical foundation; and

(f) a responsible and alert citizen.

The Estimates Committee[3] (1971) of the Fifth Lok Sabha (the Lower House of Indian Parliament) which reviewed the workers' education programme in its report, stated that the aim of workers' education was primarily to equip the workers' for trade union work and to enable them to contribute to better productivity in the national interest. It also suggested to review the scheme.

In pursuance of the recommendations of the Estimates Committee, the Government of India, appointed another Committee on Workers' Education to be headed by a veteran trade unionist G. Ramanujam. This Committee, popularly known as Review Committee[4] (1975) assessed the scheme and suggested that much needs to be done to improve not only the effectiveness of workers' education, but also give "new direction" to the scheme and its aims and objectives. The committee in its recommendations in regard to formulating the objectives for workers' education felt that since the four objectives of the workers' education as enunciated by the board in its various publications have neither been specifically mentioned in the rules and regulations of the Central Board for Workers' Education nor in Workers' Education Scheme itself, they do not adequately express the objectives of the scheme."

The Ramanujam Committee further observed that the Workers' Education should underline the need for unity among workers and the need for a single trade union movement. Workers' education, therefore, should highlight this aspect adequately and help develop in workers' broader outlook and provide them with proper perspective on workers unity and its advantages.

According to the committee, workers' education should help workers in cultivating healthy attitude towards their responsibilities and obligations, as also to the industry and the community. It should prepare the workers for a wider socio-economic understanding and participation in economic and social decision-making process at different levels.

The Ramanujam Committee after reviewing the scheme clearly visualised that its objectives, need reorientation and restatement and recommended the following six objectives for workers' education.

"Our efforts would be to give the workers an integrated education about our country, about industry, about trade unions, about industrial relations, including participative

Table 2.1

Old Objectives	New Objectives
1. to develop stronger and more effective trade unions through better trained officials and more enlightened members;	1. to equip all sections of workers', including rural Workers', for their intelligent participation in social and economic development of the nation in accordance with its declared objectives;
2. to develop leadership from the rank and file and promote the growth of democratic process and traditions in trade union organisations and administration;	2. to develop among workers a greater understanding of the problems of their social and economic environment, and their rights and obligations as citizens, as workers in industry, and as members and officials of their trade unions;
3. to equip organised labour to make its place in a democratic society and to fulfill effectively its social and economic functions and responsibilities;	3. to develop leadership from among the rank and file of workers themselves;
4. to promote among workers a greater understanding of their privileges and obligations as union members and officials and as citizens.	4. to develop strong and more responsible trade unions through more enlightened members and better trained officials;
	5. to strengthen democratic process and traditions in the trade union movement;
	6. to enable trade unions themselves to take over ultimately the functions of workers' education.

management in the organised sector, and general improvement in the quality of life of the workers. Our educational programmes would also lay increasing emphasis on the need for cooperative efforts between labour and management to improve discipline, efficiency and productivity... for the community as a whole which has to be served without interruption with quality goods and services at a reasonable cost" (Ramanujam, 1981)[5].

He further observed ... "a new culture in industrial relations will reform all our future activities. It is imperative that it is not merely enough if workers alone educated but persons in managerial and supervisory positions too will have to be simultaneously educated. Therefore, it was felt we should introduce some 'co-education programmes' for these two arms of the industry".

The new objectives suggested by the Review Committee have been accepted and incorporated in 1981. The new objectives laid greater emphasis on the involvement of labour in economic development, on the obligations and responsibilities of workers, and development of responsible trade unions. The new objectives seek to sensitise the workers more to their obligations towards the community rather than training in methods for achieving their sectional ends.

Kakkar[6] (1973) who studied the scheme in 1967 after ten years of its introduction, through a mailed questionnaire, covering 15 regional centres, found that the facilities for unit level classes were not sufficient. Dwelling on the lack of suitable accommodation for classes he said that some times classes were conducted in the premises of the industry, sometimes in the workers' residential colonies and at times in parks also. He discovered that 53.0 per cent of the worker teachers did not organise unit level classes. The arrangements for supervising the unit level classes were also very poor, resulting in bogus reports from worker-teachers. He also observed that bigger industries sponsored more worker teachers to the worker-teacher training, whereas small industries do not sponsor worker-teachers with the same enthusiasm.

Some of the important findings of the study were that workers' education programmes helped workers to think rationally and was effective in changing the external leadership system in trade unions to a greater extent. The programme enabled many workers to achieve higher positions in socio-economic hierarchy as well as in trade unions. He suggested that the schemes have to be designed in consultation with the representatives of the workers and changes in the patterns of financing and time off ought to be introduced. The study specified that the strength of the unit level classes should not be more than 15 and called for greater association with the universities. The other recommendations include incentives to the participants, longer training period, better facilities and time-off, syllabi which aimed at personality development, more use of audio-visual aids, involvement of more women workers' and favourable attitude of employers.

Taking note of the dominant position of the government in the composition of the Central Board for Workers' Education, Kakkar recommended for greater representation for unions in the regional boards. This is to enable the trade unionists to understand and implement the scheme at the local level. Non delegation of financial powers to the Education Officers, poor service conditions and lack of motivation are the main impediments for the effective functioning of the Education Officers. Also the dual responsibilities of persuading the worker-teacher for conducting the classes and inspect the classes of those worker-teachers, reduces their power of control. In the first instance, there should be mutual understanding between the worker trainees and worker-teacher. Such a reciprocal and healthy understanding is required between the Education Officers and other functionaries in the upper rungs of the ladder including the Chairman. Apart from lack of infrastructural facilities mentioned, at the unit level classes, Kakkar made the following observation:

> "At the end, a formal examination is held and almost all the workers' are declared successful". In view of the fact that women do not take much interest in the trade union activities, trade unions do not sponsor their names for training as worker-teachers. The

induction of women worker-teachers is important since they are in a better position for teaching women workers at unit level classes. Only a fraction of the work force could attend the unit classes and also the pattern of expenditure over workers' education by the trade unions, is paltry.

The hypothesis that workers' education made the strong trade unions stronger and weak trade unions weaker, is supported by Kakkar. He, however, stressed that the future of modern industrial India lies basically, to a certain extent, on the successful implementation of the workers' educational programmes.

Swaraj Bandopadyay[7] (1977) conducted a case study collecting data from the establishments under Calcutta and Barackpore Regional centres. He evaluated the performance of the scheme by interviewing a cross section of workers, worker-teachers, untrained workers, trade unionists and management personnel. The study has assessed the impact on four aspects, *viz.*, productivity mindedness, labour management relations, awareness of rights and duties and discipline consciousness. The respondents who included both trained and untrained workers perceived some consistent improvement in the four areas while those respondents who included worker teachers, unionists and managerial personnel differed considerably while rating the trained workers. They observed that although there was consistently fair improvement in the four areas, there was still an absence of cohesion between the improvement of rights and duties and labour management relations, *i.e.*, those who improved in the area concerning rights and duties did not show a proportionate improvement in other areas and vice-versa.

Sarma[8] (1980) studied the implementation of the scheme in two industrial units in Bombay to find out reasons for workers joining the scheme, and the impact of the scheme. His study, which covered a sample of worker-trainees, worker-teachers, supervisors and union officials, found that the educational levels of majority of workers were high and they were more experienced than their counterparts (untrained workers). They enrolled in the scheme to acquire knowledge and the trained workers were found to be taking more interest in trade union affairs and were more conscious about their rights compared to untrained workers. He suggested that initiative, interest and involvement of management staff are essential prerequisites for the wider acceptance of the scheme and the syllabus should be made more flexible to suit the needs of different groups of workers' in the industry. He also recommended for sponsoring workers with right aptitude, attitude, and abilities for the worker-teacher training course.

Alhah Mahar's[9] thesis (1981) entitled "A critical study of the Workers' Education Scheme in India with special reference to their role in Government of India Press" was an attempt to investigate the Role of Workers' Education Scheme in creating trade union consciousness among the workers and also for developing better industrial relations in governmental organisations. Data were obtained from 1810 workers, 43 worker teachers of seven establishments. The study found that Workers' Education Scheme was well received in Government of India Press. Trade union consciousness, safety consciousness and a sense of belonging to the organisations were the outcomes of the schemes. The scheme developed keen interest among worker-teachers with regard to the trade union activities, confidence to address union meetings, working for membership drive, etc. The Workers Education Schemes checked intervention of outside leaders in the trade union activities.

Devaki Devi[10] (1983) who evaluated the Workers' Education Scheme in Visakhapatnam region found that worker-teachers rose to higher positions in trade unions after their exposure and involvement in Workers' Education Scheme. She also claimed that training under Central Board for Workers' Education enabled worker-teachers to gain more knowledge and resulted in their personality development.

The investigation of Rizvi and Khan's[11] (1984) on the impact of Workers' education, revealed that it has reduced absenteeism, labour turnover and tardiness (84.0 per cent), and developed discipline consciousness in worker-teachers (96.0 per cent), and productivity consciousness (48.0 per cent). It also reported that there is behavioural change in 94.3 per cent of the worker-teachers, and membership in unions increased after the training and other positive aspects.

Virmani[12] (1986) conducted a study of the Workers' education in collaboration with Friedrich Elbert Foundation, West Germany. The data for the study were collected from 53 worker-teachers, 29 trade unions, 130 managements representatives, 7 training institutions, and ten organisations were selected for an indepth study. Worker-teachers from different regions were selected at random and a mailed questionnaire was administered to elicit information. The study came to the following conclusions.

1. The top managements in almost all the organisations are either indifferent or ignorant about the workers' education scheme. Only junior officers are delegated for the purpose.
2. The selection of worker-teachers is not based on the criteria of being a good teacher.
3. Both unions and managements feel that curriculum is biased against each other.
4. Substantial number of workers' are not even aware of the programme.
5. The all-India tour continues to be an attraction to the workers' in joining the scheme.
6. Management and unions are not cooperating with the scheme.
7. Lack of capable and committed worker-teachers, who can undertake unit level classes.

Virmani noted that while the number of trainees in industrial unit level classes declined from 1980 onwards, there was a remarkable increase in the number of workers in rural workers camps. (The grant-in-aid scheme to the unions has only marginal impact in the increase of workers trained. The number of unions receiving grant-in-aid also came down from the 1979-80 level). He also pointed out that the fixation of targets by the headquarters of Central Board for workers' Education, regarding different types of programmes, including unit level classes for education officers at the regional level, adversely affected the quality of the programmes. There were allegations that the figures were inflated on paper to satisfy the targets set by the higher authorities. Worker teachers received honorarium without taking the unit level classes, and the education officers never took note of such allegations. In addition, the training of workers is considered as a one-shot affair. A similar approach is adopted for the worker teacher also. He observed "very rarely, conscious efforts are made to ensure that adult education and training do not remain a one-shot affair". Such a procedure goes against the principles of education. The discouraging situation of the scheme can be attributed to emphasis on the quantitative targets, without the requisite personnel for manning them through individualised approach. Such a state of affairs is in contrast with the experience of workers' education in other countries, particularly the Anglo-Saxon group where the study circles are treated as the base on which regular programmes for workers' are conducted.

Virmani suggested the restructuring of the Workers' Education Scheme into some sort of a modular form, designed to train the trainees systematically and progressively starting from basics to intermediate courses. As a result the workers and trade unionists can broaden their perceptions and develop their skills before they proceed to advanced courses aimed at leadership training. Only promising members who have been identified in the basic courses should qualify for intermediate and higher level courses.

Virmani suggested altogether new objectives for the Workers' Education Scheme. They are as follows:

1. Improve literacy and remove ignorance;
2. make the workers'/trade unions conscious of their role in the development of the economy and the country;
3. develop a democratic, independent and strong trade union movement devoted to workers' cause, free from day-to-day political interventions;
4. prepare workers to participate effectively in the decision-making process of the enterprises;
5. check abuse of power by employers, trade union

leaders and government functionaries through healthy workers' movement;

6. make workers' conscious of their rights as well as obligations to their fellow workers' and the society as a whole;
7. change and broaden one's outlook on life.

Unnithan Sivapalan[13] (1990) (in his doctoral dissertation) submitted to the University of Kerala on the workers' education programme in Kerala, sought to ascertain the scope of workers' education programme in Kerala, to identify the bottlenecks and facilities involved in the implementation of the programme, and to find out the involvement of trade unions and the managements in programme implementation. He collected data from the regional centres of the state covering 92 worker-teachers and 968 workers by a mailed questionnaires. Data were collected from the workers who had undergone training in unit level classes and also from workers teachers by administering questionnaires.

He found that all the workers joined the scheme for the sake of knowledge. Workers with rural background and less education were interested in the programme. Supervision facilities were poor at the unit level classes and library facilities and infrastructural facilities were not sufficient. Guest lectures were given by trade union leaders and officials at the unit level classes. Involvement of voluntary organisations was very less. The programme was seriously affected by trade union rivalries, lack of funds, time and interest among management. A major outcome of the Workers' Education Scheme was the harmonious relationship between employers and employees. Awareness on industry, civic sense, general knowledge, knowledge about the functioning of trade unions, healthy life, etc., were the outcome of unit level classes. From the management perspective, the programme helped in solving labour problems in the industry. It created feelings of responsibility, etc. However, some of the managements felt, that the programme resulted in indiscipline and negative attitude towards the industry.

In an empirical study of workers' education on industrial workers Saxena and Parmar[14] (1996) found that 91.1 per cent of the sample examined by them joined the scheme of workers' education as it would help them in their personality improvement. Those who displayed self awareness about their individual role performance constituted 43.4 per cent of the sample while 57.8 per cent responded that they would undertake responsibility in relation to their role performance. A majority of the respondents felt that relation with the organisation in the social environment will be given better understanding by the training.

Mathew George[15] (1996) found the impact of workers' education programme was positive. He found 11 out of 12 worker teachers in his study rose to higher positions in unions and workers were taking active interest in union affairs productivity education improved and it contributed to the reduction of absenteeism.

The Central Board for Workers' Education itself conducted various studies, which they prefer to call "impact studies" or diagnostic studies, in collaboration with the managements and trade unions in more than 50 units. A close examination of some of those studies is relevant in this context.

The first of the diagnostic studies series was held in the Government Central Press[16] (1969) Bombay. The worker-teachers, trained and untrained workers in the industry, the management personnel and the trade unions were interviewed to know the impact of workers' education on workers, their attitude towards productivity, consciousness of trade unionism, industrial peace, qualities of leadership and workers awareness of the happenings in society.

The findings of the study can be summed up as follows:

1. By the large the scheme has succeeded in creating trade union consciousness among trained workers and the trade union is cooperating in the successful implementation of the programme.

(*a*) the training has created an environment for workers' participation in the functioning of the press;

(*b*) created a sense of belongingness and positive attitude towards their work;

(*c*) received high level of co-operation of the trade union for the progress of the Workers' Education Scheme;

(*d*) emphasis given on trade unionism has satisfied the trade unions.

Another diagnostic study was conducted in the Indian Rare Earths Ltd., Udyogmandal[17] (1969). This study, which had similar objectives as the one conducted in the Government Central Press, Bombay, included a committee represented by Kalamassery Regional Centre of Workers' Education Scheme, Management and Workers. The major findings of the study are—

1. A positive attitude towards Workers' Education Scheme in the development of trade union consciousness. Utilization of worker-teachers for sustaining trade union consciousness through the organisation of study circles and discussion groups.
2. Awareness towards family planning programmes increased due to the courses organised by the workers' education scheme.
3. Training in workers' education has motivated the workers for taking active roles in the co-operative societies.
4. Increase in the sense of responsibility and belongingness to the industry due to the training imparted by the Workers' Education Scheme.
5. The Central Board for Workers' Education can help in having the leadership qualities among the rank and file of the workers. Trade unions can look upon Central Board of Workers' Education for advice.

A similar study in the Calcutta State Transport Corporation[18] (1969) was conducted by Central Board of Workers' Education.

The major findings of the study are Workers' Education increased awareness about the happenings in the industry; developed self-esteem and positive attitude towards industry, participation in co-operatives; and lack of effective linkage of workers' education to productivity. It suggested the need for incorporating the topics related to the interest of workers in the training modules; organisation of short-term courses in industry for education officers of Workers' Education Scheme, who undertake training for worker-teachers and replacement of long-term part-time unit level classes by short-term full-time courses of two to three weeks duration.

Another diagnostic study conducted in Binod Mills Company Ltd., Ujjain[19] (1969) revealed that the scheme had developed leadership qualities, awareness of laws and regulations, skills, etc. It wanted more opportunities to be given to the worker-teachers to utilise their knowledge acquired through the programme, more incentives to the worker, better study tours and well equipped classrooms. The study also disclosed that the worker-teachers were well aware of the trade union philosophy and practice, and the management took interest in the workers' education programme.

Regional Workers' Education Centre of Mechef (Chennai) with the collaboration of EID Parry Management conducted a similar study in M/s EID Parry Ltd.[20] (1969). The impact of the scheme was studied under the joint auspices of the industry and the Regional Workers' Education Centre. The scheme thus helped to develop trade union consciousness among the workforce and the management felt that the attitude of the workers should change for better industrial relations and augmenting productivity in the industry. Thus the scheme of workers' education has been perceived differently by management and workers.

The study in the TISCO[21] (1969) groups of collieries in Dhanbad has given a better picture on the Workers' Education Scheme. The workforce, though quite large, with 12,000 strength has preserved good industrial relations. The Workers' Education Scheme got good support from the management. It was reported that the scheme could improve trade union consciousness and awareness of family welfare. Participation in trade union activities, and the influence on the productivity are the other positive results of the programme. Considerable improvement in the industrial relations was also noticed. It was suggested that for effective implementation of the scheme, full time intensive courses of three weeks duration may be conducted and incentives may also be given for the successful worker trainees. The performance of worker teachers may be considered for their promotions.

The workers' education programme was introduced in the Bharat Heavy Electricals Ltd.,[22] Hyderabad from very early stage. The impact of the Workers' Education Scheme was sought to be evaluated by the management representative and the Workers' Education Board of Hyderabad region. It found that the management was helpful in increasing the period of instruction from 30 minutes to 45 minutes a day; the influence of workers' education was felt on the various facets of the industry. The committees like grievance procedure, staff canteen, sanitation, safety, sub-evaluation, etc., had more trained worker-teachers and the programme has developed workers' trade union consciousness, and suggestions for better training were put forward by both the workers' and the management.

Misra[23] (1985) in his study of the performance of the Central Board of Workers' Education sub-regional centre examined the impact of workers' education as perceived by the worker-teachers. Various aspects of industrial relations and the impact of workers' education on them were focussed. The major findings of the study are that a better understanding between the management and workers with organisations was noticed. It developed self-confidence, ability for self-expression and other aspects of the personality of the worker. The scheme resulted in a positive attitude towards the industry and its management.

Mukherjee[24] (1985) found several success stories in workers' Education Programme. In one such programme, the training induced some of the worker trainees from a consumer goods manufacturing company, who were members of different unions, to form a single union among the workers in their factory and secure recognition from management and other benefits. In the Engineering Department, the worker-trainees and the worker-teachers were able to convince their fellow workers to look into the legalities of their lightening strike and called off the strike after getting an assurance from the management that they would be provided opportunity for undergoing training under the scheme.

Mukherjee also described the upward mobility of the worker teacher in a shipbuilding organisation in the public sector, from an ordinary member to become General Secretary of the Union. In a Public Sector Transport Organisation, a worker-teacher rose to the level of Vice-President of the Union.

In 1996, the CBWE[25] conducted a comprehensive impact study of workers' education eliciting views of trade unions, managements, management representatives, worker teachers, from all over the country. Most of the trade unions felt that the workers' education scheme has created favourable conditions for the trade unions through awareness building programmes. The management respondents viewed workers' education scheme as a tool for human resource development, attitudinal change towards work and commitment in a positive manner. Also the programmes are tailor made for personality development of individuals and development of rational and less obstructionist in approach. The management representatives also commended the workers' education scheme as value adding, purposive and awareness building mechanism. They provided useful information about family welfare and other social aspects. The joint programmes involving workers, supervisors/management cadres were more useful for developing harmonious industrial relations. The trained worker-teachers felt that workers' education scheme has helped them in participating actively both as members and office-bearers of their respective unions in the areas of Union Administration, correspondence, meetings, conferences, membership drive, cooperatives, education, productivity, quality and other behavioural and technical subjects offered by workers' education scheme.

While most of the impact studies of the CBWE emphasised the positive aspects of the scheme, we have Palekar[26] (1962) who decried that "the type of education provided under the present scheme is perfunctory and it may inculcate in the mind of worker, a secret resentment against his being a manual worker". He further, stated that like other less urgent problems, workers' education gives breathing time to the government by distracting attention of workers and trade union leaders from more urgent and vexatious problems.

While the diagnostic studies of the board revealed that there has been greater cooperation from the management and trade union leaders for the implementation of the Workers' Education Scheme, Pant[27] (1973) points out that even a large undertaking like the Railways with more than one lakh employees send one worker at a time. He opined that the union leaders were indifferent towards the scheme while workers generally considered it as a paid holiday in a new form.

According to the Indian National Trade Union Congress[28] (INTUC) (1965) the workers' education programme has not promoted the workers understanding of the economic and other working details of their own industry and hence the statistics regarding the number of teachers do not represent their progress in the field. The committee also felt that the impact of workers' education programme on productivity was not discernable where even a majority of workers attended the programme.

The Committee on Workers' Education of the National Commission on Labour Observed "most of the unions did not feel that the worker-teachers who returned to do union work have improved their capacity as a result of the training (1967)"[29].

The report of the sub-committee of the Regional Advisory Committee, Bombay (1967)[30] stated that all the trade unions have agreed that trained worker-teachers do not acquire necessary skills for organising the workers and, therefore, they do not become better trade unionists. Secondly the printed syllabus was lacking in trade union orientation. These observations and findings are contrary to the reports of the CBWE reports which claim a very positive impact of the scheme.

P.G. Hopkins[31], a UK expert in workers' education visited India in 1968 and observed the functioning of 20 unit level classes. After discussions with the concerned workers and functionaries, he was impressed by the high academic quality and the commitment of the full time professional staff of the Central Board for Workers' Education and termed the workers' education scheme in India as 'matchless' in the world". However he was critical of the scheme on several grounds.

1. The Central Board for Workers' Education implements the Government/Congress Party/INTUC/employees agenda.
2. It is over uniform and stereotyped.
3. The syllabus is too narrow in conception as it is designed by the government.
4. It lacks spontaneity, and
5. It concentrates on the universities as the alternative bodies resulting in inadequate attention to academic standards.

Styler[32] (1966), evaluated the scheme in a different way. He argued that despite the criticism that the scheme is too uniform and has no place for local variations, in Indian situation it is only efficient machinery which produces quick results in any area of activity.

From a trade union representative's view point, Sidhanta[33] (1985), denounced the confinement of workers' education largely to the organised sector, who already have some channel to air their grievances, while a large segment of work force which include the unorganised urban workers, rural poor and women workers are left unattended.

Need for the Study

Review of the studies on workers' education revealed that majority of the studies concentrated on assessing the impact of the workers' education programme on workers (who underwent training in the unit level classes) in terms of productivity, trade union consciousness, industrial relations and leadership qualities without any assessment of the pre-training knowledge levels of the workers.

Another area in which the studies were found to be lacking is that they emphasized too much on leadership.

They failed to analyse the relevance and adequacy of the syllabus and did not examine their congruence with the aims of the scheme. The training component of the Workers' Education Scheme did not figure in any of the studies.

All these studies focussed on worker-trainees and on their perception of the impact, thus neglecting the worker-teacher on whose shoulders the responsibility of conducting unit level classes and imparting education rests. Since the worker-teacher plays a vital role in the workers education continuum, the present study focusses specifically on the worker-teacher and his perceptions on the various aspects of the programme, thus making an attempt to fill the gap in the existing literature on this subject.

References

1. Virmani, B.R. (1986) *Evaluation of Workers' Education Programme* (unpublished report), Administrative Staff College of India, Hyderabad, p. 16.
2. Govt. of India (1969) *A Report of the National Commission on Labour*, Ministry of Labour, Employment and Rehabilitation, Chapter VIII, pp. 82-92.
3. Govt. of India (1971) *Estimates Committee Fourth Report*, Ministry of Labour and Rehabilitation (Dept. of Labour and Employment) Workers' Education Programme, Lok Sabha Secretariat, p. 14.
4. Ramanujam, G. (1975) *Report of the Review Committee on Workers' Education*, CBWE, Nagpur.
5. Ramanujam, G. (1981) *Workers' Education—New Vistas*, CBWE, Nagpur, pp. 8-10.
6. Kakkar N.K. (1973) *Workers' Education in India*, New Delhi: Sterling Publications.
7. Swaraj Bandyopadhyay (1977) "Impact of Workers' Education—A case study," Workers' Education: Central Board of Workers' Education, Nagpur, pp. 39-45.
8. Sarma A.M. (1980) "Workers' Education Scheme—An Evaluation," *The Indian Journal of Social Work*, Vol. XLI, July, No. 2, pp. 123-133.
9. Alhah Mahar (1981) *A Critical Study of Workers' Education Scheme in India* (with special reference to its role in Government of

India Press) (unpublished thesis) in Buch, M.B. (Ed.) Third Survey of Research in Education, NCERT, New Delhi (1986).

10. Devaki Devi, P. (1983) "Worker Teachers Lead the Trade Unions: Impact of Workers' Education", *Workers' Education*, Nagpur, p. 27.
11. Rizvi P.H. & Khan M.A. (1984) *UGC Research Project on Impact of Workers' Education, Workers' Education*, June, pp. 19-21.
12. Virmani, B.R. (1986) *Evaluation of Workers' Education Programme* (unpublished report), Administrative Staff College of India, Hyderabad, p. 16.
13. Unnithan Sivapalan T.R. (1990) "An Enquiry into the Workers' Education Programme in Kerala with a view to suggest improvements" Unpublished Thesis, Universityof Kerala.
14. Saxena, S.B. and Parman, M.N. (1996) *Impact of Workers Education on Industrial Workers*, Workers' Education, September, pp. 8-14.
15. Mathew, George (1996) *Workers' Education in Cannamore Spinning and Weaving Mills*, Workers Education, Sept., pp. 36-49.
16. Chansarkar, M.A. (Ed.)(1969) *A Diagnostic Study, Impact of Workers'*, Bombay: Education in Government Central Press, Nagpur, CBWE.
17. Chansarkar, M.A. (Ed.) (1969) *A Diagnostic Study, 'Impact of Workers' Education in the Indian Rare Earths Ltd.*, Udyogamandal, Nagpur: CBWE.
18. Chansarkar, M.A. (Ed.) (1969) *A Diagnostic Study: Impact of Workers' Education in Calcutta State Road Transport Corporation*, Calcutta Nagpur, CBWE.
19. Chansarkar, M.A. (Ed.) (1969) *A Diagnostic Study: Impact of Workers' Education in Binod Mills Co. Ltd.*, Ujjain, Nagpur, CBWE.
20. Chansarkar, M.A. (Ed.) (1969) *A Diagnostic Study: Impact of Workers' Education in E.I.D. Parry Ltd.*, Ranipet, Tamil Nadu, Nagpur: CBWE.
21. Chansarkar, M.A. (Ed.) (1969) *A Diagnostic Study: Impact of Workers' Education in TISCO Group of Collieries (Dhanbad)*, Nagpur CBWE.
22. Chansarkar, M.A. (Ed.) (1969) *Impact of Workers' Education in Bharat Heavy Electricals Ltd., Hyderabad, CBWE*, Nagpur, p. 2.

23. Misra, A.C. (1985) *National Seminar on Workers' Education in the Next Decade*, New Delhi 9-11 July, 1985 Background papers, Nagpur, Central Board for Workers' Education, pp. 2-3.
24. Mukherjee (1985) *Workers' Education in India: Some Recollections*, Workshop on Workers Education in India, organised by the Administrative Staff College of India, Hyderabad, July.
25. Chansarkar, M.A. (1966) *Impact of Workers' Education*, Workers Education, CBWE, Dec., pp. 14-25.
26. Palekar, S.A. (1962) *Problems of Wage Policy for Economic Development* (231) quoted in S.C. Pant, *Indian Labour Problems*, Allahabad, Chaitanya Publishing House.
27. Pant, S.C. (1973) *Indian Labour Problems*, Chaitanya Publishing House, Allahabad, p. 231.
28. Indian National Trade Union Congress (1965) *Labour Policies and Programmes in Fourth Five Year Plan*, Chapter II, INTUC Publication, New Delhi.
29. Govt. of India (1967) *Report of the Committee on Workers Education*, National Commission on Labour, Ministry of Labour and Employment & Rehabilitation, New Delhi, p. 14.
30. CBWE (1967) *Report of the Evaluation of the Sub-committee of the Regional Advisory Committee*, Bombay, p. 34.
31. Hopkins, P.G.H. (1968) *Workers' Education in India*, CBWE, Nagpur, March, p. 6.
32. Styler, W.E. (1966) *Adult Education in India*, Oxford University Press, London.
33. Sidhanta, T.N. (1985) "Workers' Education: A Trade Union Representative's View Point", *Indian Journal of Adult Education*, May, Vol. 46, No. 5, pp. 14-15.

3

Research Methodology

The Workers' Education Scheme has been subjected to critical evaluation from time to time. A comprehensive review of research and literature, which is a prelude to the present study, has been made.

Review of the studies on workers education revealed that majority of the studies concentrated on assessing the impact of the workers' education programme on workers (who underwent training in the unit level classes) in terms of productivity, trade union consciousness, industrial relations and leadership qualities without any assessment of the pre-training knowledge levels of the workers.

Another area in which the studies were found to be lacking is that they emphasized too much on leadership, even though the syllabus of the scheme is not aimed specifically for leadership training. Majority of the studies claimed that the worker-teachers occupied leadership positions in trade unions after the training and attributed their ascendancy in trade union hierarchy to the training, without verifying their positions in the union before they underwent training.

A common drawback of all these studies is that they failed to analyse the relevance and adequacy of the syllabus and did not examine their congruence with the aims of the scheme. The training component of the Workers' Education Scheme did not figure in any of the studies.

All these studies focussed on worker-trainees and on their perception of the impact, thus neglecting the worker-teacher on whose shoulders the responsibility of conducting unit level classes and imparting education rests. The progress, whatsoever, made by the board in the field of workers education is the result of efforts of the worker-teachers. Since the worker-teacher plays a vital role in the workers education continuum, the present study focusses specifically on the worker-teacher and his perceptions on the various aspects of the programme, thus making an attempt to fill the gap in the existing literature on this subject.

As the existing studies were limited in focus, aims, methods, the universe and sample, the researcher tried to make the study more broad based by covering a larger sample of worker-teachers and other functionaries *viz.* worker-trainees, trade union officials and management personnel concerned with the workers education scheme.

The Study

The main thrust of the present study is on the perception of the worker-teachers towards the effectiveness of workers education scheme by eliciting their opinions/views about the various aspects of the scheme.

To study the perceptions of the worker-teachers a theoretical framework was evolved through review of relevant literature on the subject. The framework included the various concepts related to the subject and its interrelationships. The objectives of the study were laid down keeping in view the theoretical framework and conceptual interrelationships.

The specific objectives of the study are:

1. To examine the socio-demographic factors associated with the training of worker-teachers and trainees;
2. to analyze the selection procedure of worker-teachers and reasons for undergoing training;
3. to study the adequacy and relevance of the syllabus being followed in the training programme;
4. to analyse various issues relating to training component in the programme;

5. to study the conduction of unit level classes and ascertain the extent of cooperation offered by the supportive organisations, *viz.*, management, trade unions and education officers;
6. to study the perceptions of worker-teachers, management personnel and trade union officials and worker trainees on various aspects of the programme and their perceived impact;
7. to offer suggestions to improve the functioning of the scheme.

Research Design

To translate the theoretical framework and conceptual interrelationships into research plan a descriptive research design was formulated. Descriptive research design was formulated with a view to describe, compare and analyse the perceptions of the worker-teachers towards the effectiveness of workers education scheme.

Research Setting

In Andhra Pradesh there are three regional centres of workers' education established in Hyderabad, Visakhapatnam and Vijayawada.

Visakhapatnam Regional Centre was selected for the study as it is the second largest city in the State of Andhra Pradesh and nerve centre of all industrial activities of coastal Andhra Pradesh. The Visakhapatnam Regional Centre has jurisdiction over four districts in which a innumerable central and state public sector units and considerable number of private sector industries like jute, sugar, alloys and paper are located. Visakhapatnam Regional Centre established in the year 1964, is second such centre in Andhra Pradesh. It has so far trained 2,410 worker-teachers and 87,160 worker trainees in the unit level classes.

Universe and Sampling Frame

The worker-teachers play a significant role in spreading

knowledge and imparting education to the workers in the industrial organisations. The total number of worker-teachers trained under orientation and refresher courses by Visakhapatnam Regional Centre during 1991-2000 was 690. Every worker-teacher who is trained by the regional centre is expected to train workers. It is estimated that in majority of the industries, a large chunk of the worker-teachers are under utilised. It shows that worker teachers are not imparting training to workers in the unit level classes. A worker-teacher who did not conduct a class or train at least one batch of workers may not know the practical problems involved in undertaking unit level classes.

This necessitated to exclude the worker-teachers who have not shown any interest in undertaking unit level classes after undergoing training in the regional centre. Hence, this study is limited to the worker-teachers who trained at least one batch of workers during 1991-2000. Application of this exclusion criterion resulted in a sampling frame of 402 worker-teachers.

Sampling

The sampling frame consists of 402 worker-teachers. As it was difficult to study all the worker-teachers owing to constraints of time and money, the study was confined to one-third of them. Therefore, a sample of 134 worker-teachers has been selected by applying sequential list method of sampling for the purpose of the present study.

As the regional centre and the industrial establishments where unit level classes are being held did not possess the data of the workers trained in the Unit Level Classes (ULC), a survey of the workers trained by the worker-teachers was undertaken with the help of the worker-teachers who were selected for this study.

A sampling frame of 2540 workers who have been trained by the worker-teachers was prepared. Out of the sampling frame, 254 workers (10 per cent) were selected by using as sample for the study by following random sampling method by selecting every tenth name in the sampling frame.

The present study has also taken into its purview the

views of trade union officials and management personnel. An inventory of trade union officials and management personnel who are familiar with the workers education programme was prepared and out of which 106 trade union officials and 120 management personnel were selected as sample for the study.

Method and Tools of Data Collection

The tools of data collection were finalised on the basis of the pre-testing. In the light of the knowledge and experience thus obtained the tools were improved upon by making necessary changes and techniques refined in order to serve the purpose of the enquiry more effectively.

The interview schedule was designed to elicit information on structural, behavioural, motivational/evaluative and attitudes of worker-teachers and worker-trainees on the various facets of workers education scheme.

The interview schedule is designed in such a way that it translated the research objectives into specific questions and thus enabled the study to obtain necessary and relevant information which appropriately explains the phenomenon.

One interview schedule and one questionnaire were prepared and administered to four types of respondents. Interview schedule was designed for eliciting information from the worker-teacher and the questionnaire was designed for collecting data from the worker trainees, union officials and management personnel. As the main focus of the study is on worker-teacher, a comprehensive interview schedule was devised to cover all the details of the workers education programme. The interview schedule for worker-teacher consists of six parts. The first part of the interview schedule consists of questions seeking information on the socio-demographic characteristics of the respondents. The second part of the schedule deals with the questions relating to his/her selection as worker-teacher. Information pertaining to the adequacy of the time allotted and relevance of the syllabus of the training programme is sought by their third part of the schedule. The fourth part includes the views of the worker-teachers on the training components like duration of training, training methodology coverage, trainee involvement and level of inputs. The fifth part contains questions relating to the conduct of unit level classes and the cooperation of the management, trade unions and education officers. The last part of the schedule contains questions seeking the views of the respondents about the programme in general and questions relating to the impact of the programme.

The questionnaire for worker-trainees, union officials and management personnel comprises two parts: Part-A consists of socio-economic background of the respondents while Part-B consists of questions relating to the general aspects of the workers education programme and their perceived impact.

In the field study for collection of data, survey techniques were employed through administration of interview schedules. However, they were not entirely relied upon. Observational methods were given due prominence in collection of the data. Also during the study elite groups and other knowledgeable persons connected with workers' education were contacted to obtain information at informal level. While some of the views expressed were highly impressionistic, subjective and products of fertile imagination, a broad spectrum of the ferment in the milieu of industrial workforce which is in the quest for industrial peace, emerged. Workers' Education viewed within the broad-frame of industrial relations, the conflicting views and expectations of the rank and file workers, the union officials, the management representatives, the development workers namely the education officers and worker-teachers in the workers education programme, the various pieces when inter-linked, a broad spectrum is discernible.

Pre-testing

A pre-testing was conducted by interviewing ten per cent of the selected sample and thus 15 worker-teachers were interviewed and the second schedule was administered to 25 worker-trainees, 10 trade union officials and 13 management personnel. In tune with the responses of the respondents to each of the questions in the interview schedule, the researcher subequently modified and finalised the sequence, content and format of the questions in the interview schedule.

Data Collection

After finalisation of the tools for collection of data and the selection of the subjects to come under study is over, the researcher administered research tools to the sample population to collect data pertaining to the study. The researcher made an attempt to contact them in their respective organisations. In the first visit the researcher met the respondents during duty hours and explained them the purpose of the study and informed them that the information obtained from them would be kept confidential. The subsequent visits were made after working hours and sometimes the researcher made home visits and collected data from the worker-teachers. The average time taken to collect data from the worker-teacher is 2 hours. In the case of second category of respondents (worker-trainees and management personnel), he met them during working hours, explained them the purpose of the study. He circulated the questionnaires and collected them next day. The trade union respondents were met in the union offices. As the respondents were familiar with the scheme and purpose of the study, the collection of data from the large sample took 6 months time from Sept. 2000 to March 2001.

Problems in Data Collection

Since the sampled respondents were spread over four districts in a range of 200 km, collection of data involved considerable time. Even though most of the respondents were cooperative, a few of them refused to answer at the first instance. After constant persuasion and assuring them that these responses would be kept confidential, they obliged to give the required information. As the study progressed the respondents were cooperative and good rapport was developed with most of them.

The secretary of one trade union refused permission to

interview trade union office-bearers of his union and he also complained that workers' education scheme has a negative influence on the workers as worker who undergoes training tries to start new union or split the existing ones. Another problem the researcher had to face was the non-availability of the respondents in the respective establishments due to shift system that operate in the organisations. Sometimes the researcher tried to contact them at their houses and they were going out on some domestic works. In some cases, the questionnaires given to them were kept aside till the researcher approached them for the questionnaires. Another union in the same industrial establishment extended maximum cooperation as its President called a meeting of the worker-teachers of his union and the union officials and allowed the researcher to freely interact with them.

During the course of data collection, some respondents thinking that the researcher was from the university enquired about improving their educational qualifications by appearing privately or through correspondence courses. The researcher assisted them by providing the required information and guidance to gain their confidence.

The researcher made frequent visits to the unit level classes sometimes along with the education officer and sometimes without the education officer. There was full attendance at the unit level class on a visit made along with the Education Officers while the second visit paid by the researcher without education officer, found thin attendance at the unit level classes.

Data Processing and Analysis

The interview schedule were pre-coded. Data collected by interview schedules were edited for any omission or errors. Then with the help of Statistical Package for Social Sciences (SPSS) the data were processed. The data were subjected to statistical analyses keeping in view the objectives of the study.

Limitations

While adequate care has been taken to make this study on

workers' education more comprehensive, however, it was not free from some limitations.

1. One of the major limitations of the study is the absence of proper data base of the workers trained in the unit level classes. Most of the employers and the regional centre do not have a proper system of records relating to workers education.
2. Though the present study is largely descriptive in nature, notwithstanding the richness of data, it lacks control of the variables which are many and impinge upon the behavioural patterns of the respondents.
3. The extent of reliability and validity of the findings of the study depend upon the usual problems of measurement of attitudes and quantification of observational methods.

Scheme of the Book

The book has eight chapters. First chapter deals with the conceptual framework of workers education and scheme of workers education in India. The second chapter reviews the earlier studies made on the subject of workers education. The research methodology forms the subject matter of the third chapter. The fourth chapter examines the socio-economic and demographic profile of the respondents. The fifth chapter analyses the perceptions of the worker-teachers and the sixth chapter examines the views of the worker-trainees, trade union officials and management personnel on different aspects of the programme. The seventh chapter throws light on the impact of the training programme by examining the views of all the respondents. The last chapter embodies the conclusions and suggestions.

4

Socio-Demographic Profile of the Respondents

In this section, an attempt is made to know the socio-economic background of the respondents. The standard variables that are usually employed to determine the socio-economic status like age, sex, experience, caste, type of the job, income and the union affiliations were taken into consideration.

SECTION - A

Worker-Teachers

As specified in the methodology chapter, the main focus of the study is on worker-teacher and his perceptions with regard to the effectiveness of the programme. Workers' education programme consists of training of worker-teachers and rank and file workers. It is an off-the job training programme conducted by the outside agency namely central board for workers' education. A sample of 134 worker teachers who underwent training and who imparted training to at least one batch of workers at the unit level classes was selected and an interview schedule was administered to them. What appears in this section is the analysis of the data relating to socio-demographic aspects of the worker-teachers, which sheds some light on the correlates of training.

Age

In all sociological studies, age is taken into consideration as it plays a fairly significant role in depicting the differences in values, views and attitudes between generations. The assumption is that difference in age, always leads to corresponding variation in the perceptions, values and role performance of the worker-teachers. In the sample, the age of the respondents ranges from 20 to 48 years while the mean age is 35.7 years. The frequency distribution of the respondents' age is presented in Table 4.1.

Table 4.1
Distribution of Respondents by Age

Age in years	*Frequency*	*Percentage*
20-30	33	24.6
31-40	73	54.5
41-50	28	20.9
Total	134	100.0

Mean 35.7 years; S.D. 6.1 years; Range - Low: 20; High: 48.

It is evident from the above table that the majority of the respondents (54.5%) belonged to the age group of 31 to 40 years, followed by the respondents in the age groups of 20 to 30 years, and 41 to 50 years (20.9%). It can be concluded that the middle aged workers are more likely to evince interest in the workers' education as it is at this age worker wants to involve herself/himself in various productive activities, carve a niche for oneself in the factory and the trade union activities. Kakkar[1] (1973) found that 52 per cent of the workers are from 20 to 30 years, while 35 per cent are from 31 to 40 years. The fact that only 21 per cent of the respondents are above 41 years indicates that with the increase in age, propensity to get trained reduces. This is in consonance with the Harley Frazis[2] (2000) finding that age after certain point reduces the incentive to training.

Sex

Sex-wise distribution of the respondents revealed that all of them are males. The presence of females is nil. This may be due to the fact that the women do not take active role in union activities, or trade unions do not sponsor them for worker-teacher training (Kakkar, 1973)[3].

Religion

Religion and caste are two important factors in the Indian social structure. Though in principle religion or caste do not prevent a person from taking up any occupation or profession, these two have been taken into consideration, to find out whether differences in religion and caste background of the respondents have any bearing on their participation in the training programme and to know which religious group is showing more interest in workers' education.

Table 4.2

Distribution of Respondents by Religion

Religion	*Frequency*	*Percentage*
Hindu	118	88.1
Muslim	11	8.2
Christian	5	3.7
Total	134	100.0

The religious background of the respondents revealed that an overwhelming majority of the respondents (88.1%) belonged to Hindu religion, followed by Muslims with eight per cent and the remaining 3.7 per cent are Christians. The domination of the Hindus is in conformity with the religious composition of the population.

Caste

Caste is an important sociological variable in India. It has been defined as homogenous community (Resely 1969)[4], hereditary membership and endogamy (Ketkar, 1909)[5] hereditary occupation (Srinivas, M.N. 1966)[6], Senart[7], (1930) considered purity of descent and purity of occupations as the main criteria of the caste system. Indian society is traditionally divided into four varnas and the jatis (caste) developed later and continued to grow in number through the extending division of labour, the incorporation of tribes, to a lesser extent. Bottomore[8] (1975), according to him "Jati is the endogamous group and principal reference group of the individual, embodying a distinctive style of life and maintaining it by the exercise of customary, judicial sanctions. The caste system is continuing its hold on the population and its continuity is a solid proof of its adaptive capacities (Sharma, 1977)[9] and the industrial workers are not insulated from caste. For the purpose of present analysis the castes are divided into four categories: Scheduled castes and tribes, other backward classes, forward castes (other castes).

Table 4.3
Distribution of Respondents by Caste

Caste	*Frequency*	*Percentage*
Forward	46	39.8
Backward	60	50.8
Scheduled Caste	12	9.4
Total	118*	100.0

* There were 118 Hindu respondents in the sample, hence N = 118 for the distribution of castes

Looking at the caste-distribution of the respondents, it can be noticed that out of the 118 Hindu respondents in the sample (apart from 11 Muslims and five Christians for whom caste is not applicable), majority of the respondents (50.8%) is from backward castes, followed by other castes (39.8%) and the scheduled castes (9.4%).

Length of Service

Length of service or work experience is one of the factors associated with the training. Theory suggests that with incease in length of service, there is little inclination towards training. It is one of the factors that influences the workers' perceptions towards trainin and its outcome.

Table 4.4
Distribution of Respondents by Experience

Length of Service	*Frequency*	*Percentage*
2 to 8 years	38	28.4
9 to 16 years	63	47.0
17 to 24 years	33	24.6
Total	134	100.0

Range: 2 to 24 years, Mean 12.3 years, S.D. 5.386

An analysis of length of service of the respondents revealed that a large number of the respondents (47%) had 9 to 16 years of work experience, followed by respondents (28.4%) with less than eight years. The remaining respondents (24.6%) had more than 16 years of experience. The experience ranges from 2 to 24 years and the mean experience of the respondents is about 12 years. It may be inferred from the data that workers with considerable service are more likely interested in improving their knowledge levels and imparting it to their fellow employees. The fact that workers with the longer tenure constituted less than one fourth of the sample indicates that with the increase in tenure, the likelihood of getting trained diminishes. It is in accordance with the theory that suggests training should decrease with tenure (Harley Frazis *et. al.* 2000)[10].

Education

In the Workers' Education Programme there are no specific educational qualifications laid down to undergo either the worker-teacher training or unit level classes. Rules of the CBWE say "among industrial worker, whether literate or illiterate, trade union members or not, and full time union officials and staff should be eligible for services provided by the board (1957)[11].

An analysis of the educational attainments of the

respondents is considered necessary to know whether the formal education has any bearing on the propensity to receive training. Lillard and Tan[12] (1986); Lynch[13] (1992), Lynch and Black[14] (1998) found that there is an association between the formal schooling and participation in training. This may be because formal schoolings lays substantive foundation upon which future training can build and it cultivates interest in learning or it lowers reluctance to engage in future training (Dave E. Marcotte, 2000)[15].

Education is positively related to the receipt and intensity of formal learning (Harley Frazis *et. al.*, 2000)[16]. Education is related to the ability to learn specific job-related skills. Higher educated workers will have higher disposition towards training as they are expected to receive more returns in training. Past research on training found a strong positive relationship between formal schooling, particularly four years of college and participation in job. (Brown, 1989)[17]

Table 4.5

Distribution of Respondents by Education

Educational Attainment	*Frequency*	*Percentage*
Below SSC	43	32.1
SSC	53	39.6
Intermediate	16	11.9
Degree	22	16.4
Total	134	100.0

From the table it is evident that a little over 32 per cent of the respondents have not completed their secondary education and hence come under the category of below SSC or Matriculation. While nearly 40 per cent hold SSC qualifications, almost 12 per cent of them possess intermediate qualification and the remaining (16.4%) are graduates. Kakkar[18] (1973) study found 72.0 per cent of the trainees had less than matriculation qualification. The fact that more educated/highly educated persons constituted only 16.4 per cent of the sample is at variance with the findings of Brown[19] (1989) that more educated receive more training. The less involvement of better educated may be due to the fact that training in workers' education do not guarantee or bring return in the form of any promotion/incremental increase in the pay. This indicates that lesser educated are more likely to receive training. The plausible reason for the high school educated workers inclination to undergo or receive training is that they look at the training as a substitute for additional schooling.

Type of Job

An analysis of the occupational background of the respondents is made to know which occupational group is evincing interest in workers' education. For the purpose of analysis the occupations/designations of the workers are classified into two types (1) blue collar workers consisting of workers engaged in the technical aspects of work, (2) white collar workers doing the non-technical work like clerks. The occupational background of the respondents is presented in the following table.

Table 4.6
Distribution of Respondents by Job

Type of Job	*Frequency*	*Percentage*
Blue collar	103	76.9
White collar	31	23.1
Total	134	100.0

The data in the above table show that the majority (76.9%) of the respondents were holding blue collar jobs, while a little over 23 per cent were white collar workers.

The above data reveal that blue-collar workers are more likely to be interested to receive training in non-technical aspects of the job and industry as their knowledge level of the above is considerably low. The selection of nominee for worker-teacher training is done by the union and the management releases the worker nominated by the union for training. The data show that the unions are more likely to see that its blue collar workers undergo training in workers' education.

Union Affiliation

Link between unions and training is potentially important and (Francis Green *et. al.*, 1999)[20]. Unions positively affect the training in many ways even though they have only an informal role in training. Unionized workers both manual and non-manual were more likely than non-unionised workers to participate in training. Venum[21] (1995) found positive coefficients on a union variable on the determinants on the job training, negatively for the off the job training.

In India the unions at the unit/plant level are loosely affiliated to national federations (National Commission on Labour[22], 1969). These national federations are affiliated to political parties. For example both the All India Trade Union Congress (AITUC), and Centre of Indian Trade Union (CITU) are the labour wings of Communist Party of India (CPI) and Communist Party of India (Marxist) (CPM) respectively. While the Indian National Trade Union Congress (INTUC) is affiliated to Indian National Congress, a Centrist Political Party and the Bharatiya Mazdoor Sangh (BMS) is the labour wing of the rightist Bharatiya Janata Party. The unions at the plant level are broadly classified under three heads based on their ideologies for the purpose of the analysis.

Table 4.7
Distribution of Respondents by Their Unions' Affiliation

Affiliation		*Frequency*	*Percentage*
Leftist Unions		32	24.0
AITUC	17		
CITU	15		
Left of Centre		74	55.1
INTUC	55		
HMS	13		
Others	6		
Rightist Unions		28	20.9
BMS			
Total		134	100.0

Leftist unions: AITUC, CITUC, Left of the Center (Centrist): INTUC, HMS, Rightist unions: BMS and others.

An analysis of the trade union affiliation to which worker-teachers belong revealed that 41 per cent of the respondents belonged to INTUC, which is labour wing of the Congress Party, followed by BMS (20.9%). While communist unionss have (both AITUC and CITU) have 24.0 per cent following among workers and Hind Mazdur Sabha (HMS) a centrist union has nearly 10 per cent of the worker-teachers as its members. Since it is a government sponsored programme, the INTUC, which is the labour wing of the Congress Party, the dominant ruling party for 45 out of 50 years of the country's independence, took advantage of the programme, and has been sponsoring more number for the worker-teacher training programme. The data show that centrist unions are more likely to nominate their workers for workers' training than the non-centrist unions and are interested in developing second line leadership in their unions. Ramaswamy[23] (1986) observed that the INTUC supported the scheme since this federation always claimed that it promotes larger social interests and not narrow sectional ones.

Income

Table 4.8
Distribution of Respondents by Income

Income Monthly (Rs.)	*Frequency*	*Percentage*
Less than 2500	25	18.7
2501 - 5000	73	54.4
5001 - 7500	32	23.9
7501 - 10000	4	3.8
Total	134	100.0

Minimum: Rs. 1800, Maximum: Rs. 10000, Mean: Rs. 4216

The monthly earnings of the worker-teachers show that the majority (54.4%) of the respondents has an income ranging from Rs. 2501 to Rs. 5000. Almost one-fourth (24 per cent) of them had become between Rs. 5001 to Rs. 7500 and the remaining (3.0%) had an income of more than Rs.

7500. The total monthly earning range from Rs. 1800 to Rs. 10000 and the average income stands at Rs. 4216.

Summary

The analysis of the socio-economic data of the worker-teachers revealed that a dominant majority of them (88.0%) are Hindus, all of them are men, more than 50 per cent belong to backward castes. Education wise the respondents are fairly educated, had considerable work experience in the industry. Occupational analysis show that majority of them are blue collared workers, with an income ranging from Rs. 1800 - Rs. 10,000 and an average income of Rs. 4216 and their unions are affiliated to centrist federation.

SECTION - B

Worker-Trainee

The last stage in the workers' education programme is the training of rank and file workers by the worker-teacher in the units or establishments. The present study covered 254 worker-trainees who underwent training in the unit level classes. This section examines the socio-demographic characteristics of the respondents who underwent training.

Sex

Table 4.9
Distribution of Respondents by Sex

Sex	*Frequency*	*Percentage*
Male	248	97.6
Female	6	2.4
Total	254	100.0

Sex-wise distribution of the respondents revealed that an overwhelming majority (97.6%) of them were men and women workers constituted only 2.4% of the sample. The unit level classes are conducted after working hours and that may discourage women workers from participating in the unit level classes. Due to the criticism on this count the board has taken several steps to increase the participation of women in the programme, like launching of worker-teacher training programme, exclusively for women. Despite such efforts the programme has not been able to attract more women workers.

The above finding is in tandem with Venum[24] (1995) who found evidence that men are more likely to receive formal company training than women. Women are more likely to experience gaps in their labour force participation than men due to childbearing and as a consequence there may be reduced incentive to train women (Harley Frazis *et. al.*, 2000)[25].

Age

Table 4.10
Distribution of Respondents by Age

Age	*Frequency*	*Percentage*
Below 31 years	30	11.8
31 to 40 years	108	42.5
41 to 50 years	116	45.6
Total	254	100.0

It is found that a large number of the respondents (45.6%) belonged to the age group of 41 to 50 years while workers in the age group of 31 to 40 years accounted for 42.5 per cent and the remaining respondents were in less than 31 years group. The data show poor participation of young workers in the programme. This may be attributed to the selection procedure of the worker-teacher who might have preferred older workers, or the disinterest of the young workers or the failure of study tour in attracting them to the programme. Age is associated with decrease in probability of being trained at the high-end of the range (Harley Frazis 2000)[26]. The data contradict the theory as majority of the workers are in the age group of 41-50 years. Compared to the age of the worker-teachers, the worker-trainees are older.

Religion

Table 4.11
Distribution of Respondents by Religion

Religion	*Frequency*	*Percentage*
Hindus	230	90.5
Muslims	14	5.5
Christians	10	3.9
Total	254	100.0

With regard to the religious background of the respondents, it is found that a large majority (90.5 per cent) of them were Hindus followed by Muslims (5.5%) and Christians (3.9%). The data are more or less in consonance with the religious composition of the nation.

Caste

Table 4.12
Distribution of Respondents by Caste

Caste	*Frequency*	*Percentage*
Forward Castes	85	35.4
Backward Castes	113	47.0
Scheduled Tribes	35	14.5
Scheduled Castes	7	3.0
Total	254	100.0

Caste is an important variable in the Indian context. Since it is a powerful social phenomenon and has permeated into the modern institutions like; industry/education and economy its impact on the behavioural patterns of individuals and functioning of the organisation is consequently felt. The caste background of the respondents revealed that a large number of the respondents (47.0%) belong to backward class, followed by forward caste respondents (35.4%) while the remaining (17.6%) belong to Scheduled Castes and Tribes. The backward class respondents are more likely to receive training than others.

Education

Table 4.13
Distribution of Respondents by Education

Educational Attainment	*Frequency*	*Percentage*
Below SSC	84	33.1
SSC	106	41.7
Intermediate	52	20.5
Degree	12	4.7
Total	254	100.0

The educational attainments of the respondents are presented in the Table. The data show that nearly one-third (33.1%) of them had not studied up to SSC, while about 42 per cent of the respondents had SSC qualifications, which is now a minimum qualification to enter into the job market. Nearly one-fifth (20.4%) of them had intermediate qualification while nearly five per cent were graduates. From the data it can be concluded that the programme of workers' education is attracting more workers with low level of education. The better educated are keeping themselves off the programme as it is off-the-job training programme as there is no monetary or career incentive for undergoing training. This finding contradicts the finding of Frazis Harley *et. al.*[27] (2000), Brown[28] (1989) that Bachelors degree holders were significantly more likely than high school graduates to receive training.

Length of Service

Work experience is one of the factors that influences the perceptions of workers. The data on work experience revealed that a majority (64.5%) of them had 10 to 20 years of work experience, while around 11 per cent of the workers had less than 10 years of service, and the remaining almost 17 per cent of them had more than 21 years of experience. This

Table 4.14
Distribution of Respondents by Experience

Experience in years	*Frequency*	*Percentage*
Below 10	47	18.5
11 - 20	164	64.5
21 - 30	43	17.0
Total	254	100.0

shows that workers with longer service in the organisations are more likely to enroll with the programme. Workers with less experience are showing poor interest in the programme or junior workers may feel that apart from having other interests to pursue, they have age on their side to join the programme at a latter stage. The data also show that only 17 per cent of the respondents have more than 20 years of experience. This shows that the receipt of training declines with tenure. This has been in consonance with the theory which suggests that training decreases with tenure (Harley Frazis *et. al.*[29]).

Type of Job

Table 4.15
Distribution of Respondents by Type of Job

Type of Job	*Frequency*	*Percentage*
Blue collared	189	74.4
White collared	65	25.6
Total	254	100.0

The data in the table indicate that nearly three-fourths (74.4%) of the respondents were of blue collared workers and the remaining 25.6 per cent were white collared workers. The data suggest that the blue collared workers are evincing interest in the programme.

Union Affiliation

Table 4.16
Distribution of Respondents by Union Affiliation

Union Affiliation	*Frequency*	*Percentage*
Leftist	66	26.0
Centrist	148	58.3
Rightist	11	4.3
Others (independent)	29	11.4
Total	254	100.0

The table shows that a majority of the respondents (58.3%) belong to centrist unions followed by leftist unions (26.0%).

Summary

The above analysis shows a majority of them are Hindu men and belong to backward castes. Educational attainments reveal that majority of them are less educated than the worker-teachers, had more work experience than worker-teachers, and blue collared belong to centrist unions.

SECTION - C

Trade Union Officials

This section analyses the socio-demographic profile of the trade union officials. A total of 106 trade union officials were selected as sample for this study.

Age

Table 4.16(A)
Distribution of Respondents by Age

Age	*Frequency*	*Percentage*
31 - 40	22	20.7
41 - 50	56	52.8
> 50	28	26.5
Total	106	100.0

Analysis of the data reveal that majority of the respondents (52.8%) belonged to the age group of 41 to 50 years and a little over one-fourth of them were above 51 years. This shows that, by and large, trade union leaders are in their late middle ages.

Education

Table 4.17
Distribution of Respondents by Education

Education	*Frequency*	*Percentage*
SSC	23	21.7
Intermediate	62	58.5
Degree & above	21	19.8
Total	106	100.0

The education attainments of the trade union leaders reveal that majority of them (58.5%) had intermediate qualification indicating that the leaders are fairly educated.

Length of Service

Table 4.18
Distribution of Respondents by Experience

Experience	*Frequency*	*Percentage*
Nil	6	5.6
1 - 10 years	48	45.3
11 - 20 years	52	30.2
21 - 30 years	20	18.9
Total	106	100.0

The analysis of data relating to work experience of the respondents shows that nearly half of them had less than ten years of experience followed by a substantial number of them having 11 to 20 years of experience. It is also pertinent to note that a few respondents (5.6%) have no experience in the industry. This indicates the presence of outsiders in the union hierarchy.

Caste

Table 4.19
Distribution of Respondents by Caste

Caste	*Frequency*	*Percentage*
Forward	35	33.0
Backward	68	54.7
SC	11	10.4
ST	2	1.9
Total	106	100.0

The caste composition of the trade union leaders shows that a majority of them (54.7%) belonged to backward classes followed by forward caste (33.0%).

Union Affiliation

Table 4.20
Distribution of Respondents by Union Affiliation

Union Affiliation	*Frequency*	*Percentage*
Leftist	66	26.0
Rightist	11	4.3
Centrist	148	58.3
Independent	29	11.4
Total	106	100.0

The affiliation pattern of the unions of the respondents shows that a majority of the respondents (58.3 per cent) belonged to centrist unions.

Sex and Religion

The religious composition of the respondents shows an overwhelming (84.9%) majority is Hindus. The sex composition shows that all of them are males. It is surprising to note that of women are absent in the trade union leadership positions. It suggests that climbing the union hierarchy is difficult for the women or the union executive positions may not be open to them.

Summary

The above analysis revealed that an overwhelming majority of them are Hindus and females in the trade union hierarchy are totally absent. The caste background of the respondents shows majority of them belonged to backward castes and are less experienced and belonged to 41 to 50 years age group. The union affiliation reveals that majority of them belong to centrist union.

SECTION - D

Management Personnel

This section examines the socio-demographic profile of the management personnel. A total of 120 management personnel were selected as sample for this study.

Age

Table 4.21
Distribution of Respondents by Age

Age	*Frequency*	*Percentage*
Below 30 years	6	5.0
31 to 40 years	39	32.5
41 to 50 years	52	43.4
50 & above	23	19.1
Total	106	100.0

Analysis of the data revealed that a substantial number of respondent (43.4%) are in age group of 31 to 40 years and nearly one-third of them are in the age group of 21 to 30 years.

Education

Education is one of the variables that determines the socio-economic status of the individual and influences the perceptions and attitudes of the individuals. Here the education attainments of the management personnel are presented in the following table.

Table 4.22
Distribution of Respondents by Education

Education	*Frequency*	*Percentage*
Intermediate	28	23.3
Degree & above	92	74.7
Total	106	100.0

The analysis of data relating to level of education of the management personnel show that three-fourths of them (74.7%) have bachelors degree and above qualifications.

Length of Service

Table 4.23
Distribution of Respondents by Experience

Experience	*Frequency*	*Percentage*
1 to 10 years	24	20.0
11 to 20 years	78	65.0
21 to 30 years	18	15.0
Total	106	100.0

The data relating to the work experience show that nearly two-third of them have 11 to 20 years of experience. This indicates that majority of them are senior management personnel.

Caste

Table 4.24
Distribution of Respondents by Caste

Caste	*Frequency*	*Percentage*
Forward	68	56.7
Backward	32	26.7
Scheduled Caste	14	11.6
Scheduled Tribe	6	5.0
Total	106	100.0

Caste composition suggests more than half of respondents (56.7%) are from forward caste.

Men constituted an overwhelming majority (97.5%) and women formed an insignificant percentage of the respondents (2.5%).

More than two-thirds of the respondents were Hindus (70.8%) a little over one-fourth of them are Christians.

Summary

An overview of the results of the above data reveal that the majority of the management respondents are Hindus and are predominately men and belong to forward caste. Education wise they are highly educated and are in the age group of 41 to 50 years with an experience of 11 to 20 years.

References

1. Kakkar, N.K. (1973) *Workers Education in India,* Sterling Publishers, New Delhi, p. 293.
2. Harley Frazis *et. al.* (2000) *Correlates of Training: An Analysis Using both Employer and Employee Characteristics,* Industrial and Labour Relations Review, Vol. 53, No. 3, April, p. 443-462.
3. Kakkar, N.K. (1973) *Workers Education in India,* Sterling Publishers, New Delhi, p. 294.
4. Resely, H.H. (1969) *The People of India,* Orient Books Reprint Corporation, Delhi.

5. Ketkar, S.V. (1909) *The History of Caste in India,* Ithaca, Tayer and Carpenter.
6. Srinivas, M.N. (1966) *Social Change in Modern India,* University of California Press, Berkeley.
7. Senart, E. (1930) *Caste in India: The Facts and the System,* Translated by S. Denison Ross, Metheun & Co., London.
8. Bottomore, T.B. (1975) *Sociology: A Guide to Problems and Literature,* Blackie & Son (India) Ltd., Bombay.
9. Sharma, K.L. (1977) *New Introduction,* Review of Caste in India by J. Murdock, Rawat Publications, Delhi.
10. Harley Frazis *et. al.* (2000) *Correlates of Training: An Analysis Using both Employer and Employee Characteristics,* Industrial and Labour Relations Review, Vol. 53, No. 3, April, p. 447.
11. CBWE (1958) *Rules of the Central Board for Workers Education,* CBWE, Nagpur.
12. Lillard *et. al.* (1996) *Private Sector Training who Gets It and What are Its Effects?* R-3331 - D02, Santa Monica, California.
13. Lynch, Lisa, M. (1992) *Private Sector Training and Earnings of Young Workers,* American Economic Review, Vol. 82, No. 1, pp. 299-312.
14. Lynch, Lisa M. and Sandra E. Black (1998) *Beyond the Incidence of Employer-Provided Training,* Industrial and Labour Relations Review, Vol. 52, No. 1, pp. 64-81.
15. Dave E. Marcotte (2000) *Continuing Education, Job Training and the Growth of Earnings Inequality,* Industrial and Labour Relations Review, Vol. 53, No. 4, July, p. 621.
16. Harley Frazis *et. al.* (2000) *Correlates of Training: An Analysis Using both Employer and Employee Characteristics,* Industrial and Labour Relations Review, Vol. 53, No. 3, April, p. 453.
17. Brown Charles (1989) *Emperical Evidence on Private Training,* In investing in people, Background papers, Vol. I, Washington DC, Commission on workforce quality and labour market efficiency, US Dept. of Labour, pp. 301-29.
18. Kakkar, N.K. (1973) *Workers Education in India,* Sterling Publishers, New Delhi, p. 295.
19. Brown Charles (1989) *Emperical Evidence on Private Training,* In investing in people, Background papers, Vol. I, Washington DC, Commission on workforce quality and labour market efficiency, US Dept. of Labour, p. 305.

20. Francis Green *et. al.* (1999) *Trade Unions and Training Practices in British Work Places,* Industrial and Labour Relations Review, Vol. 52, No. 2, pp. 179-195.
21. Venum, Jonathan (1995) *Sources of Training and Their Impact on Wages*, Industrial and Labour Relations Review, Vol. 48, pp. 812-826.
22. Govt. of India (1969) *National Commission on Labour,* Ministry of Labour, Govt. of India, p. 335.
23. Ramaswamy, E.A. (1986) *Towards an Enlightened Workforce,* Business India, Dec. p. 32.
24. Venum, Jonathan (1995) *Sources of Training and Their Impact on Wages*, Industrial and Labour Relations Review, Vol. 48, p. 815.
25. Harley Frazis *et al.* (2000) *Correlates of Training: An Analysis Using Both Employer and Employee Characteristics,* Industrial and Labour Relations Review, Vol. 53, No. 3, April, p. 445.
26. *Ibid.*, p. 448.
27. *Ibid.*, p. 452.
28. Brown Charles (1989) *Emperical Evidence on Private Training,* In investing in people, Background papers, Vol. I, Washington DC, Commission on Workforce Quality and Labour Market Efficiency, US Dept. of Labour, p. 305.
29. Harley Frazis *et. al.* (2000) *Correlates of Training: An Analysis Using Both Employer and Employee Characteristics,* Industrial and Labour Relations Review, Vol. 53, No. 3, April, p. 450.

5

Effectiveness of Workers' Education Scheme: Perception of Worker-Teachers

The Central Board for Workers' Education was established to administer and implement a countrywide Workers' Education Programme with well defined objectives to develop strong and more effective trade unions through well trained officials and more enlightened members. It was also aimed at promoting among workers a greater understanding of the problems of their economic environment and to develop leadership from the rank and file of the workers.

For achieving these objectives, the board developed a need-based three tier-training programme. In the first stage, the education officers, are recruited by the board and given training. After completion of the training they will be posted to the regional centers spread over throughout India. In the second stage the education officers will train workers at the regional level for a period of three months. The workers who undergo training are known as worker-teachers as they have to train their fellow workmen. In the third stage the worker-teachers have to impart training in their respective units to the workers in what are known as unit level classes. The worker-teacher is link between the board and the workers at the unit level. He plays pivotal role in spreading the knowledge to the workers. Here an attempt is made to study the effectiveness of the workers' education programme at the Visakhapatnam Regional Centre by focussing on the perceptions of the worker-teachers and other functionaries. The study confines itself to the worker-teachers who have taken/trained at least one batch of workers at the unit level classes during the study period of 10 years in the establishments that come under the Visakhapatnam regional centre. A total of 403 worker-teachers have undertaken unit level classes in the region during the last ten years and out of which one-third is taken as sample for the purpose of the present study. The sample consists of 134 worker-teachers and the perceptions of the respondents are presented in this chapter.

This chapter, which presents the results of the data collected from worker-teachers is sub-divided into five sections. The first section deals with the perceptions of worker-teachers on selection procedure and second section analyses the views about syllabus. Their perceptions of training component have been described in section three. The fourth section examines their views on unit level classes. And the last section deals with the perceptions of the respondents about the general aspects of the scheme.

SECTION - A

Selection Procedure

The regional centres notify the trade unions and employers about the training courses. The workers are sponsored by the trade unions and the employers release the workers for training. There is no hard and fast rule with regard to the selection procedure and what is of importance to the regional centre is the availability of the worker for the training programme. Different managements follow different criteria for selection. Generally selection of the worker is left to the trade unions and the management is to permit the worker nominated by the union to undergo training. The present study makes an attempt to throw light on the selection procedure evolved by different industries as perceived by the worker-teachers.

The views of workers about the people who selected them for worker-training show that a majority of them (59%)

Table 5.1
Distribution of Respondents by Their Perceptions About Selection Method

Perception About Selection Method	*Frequency*	*Percentage*
Union sponsorship	79	59.0
Personal request to the union	16	11.9
Management sponsorship	13	9.7
Personal request to the management	2	1.5
Joint decision (union and management)	24	17.9
Total	134	100.0

informed that their union selected them, followed by joint decision of the management and union (17.9%). Personal requests to the management (11.9%) and the management on its own nominating the worker without any role of the union constituted around 10 per cent which is not at all significant. In all the 90 per cent cases the union played a crucial role in the selection of the workers. Since it is a programme meant for educating the workers, organised by an outside government agency, the management content to play second fiddle in the programme. The finding that it is the union that has the major 'say' in the selection procedure has been corroborated by Virmani's[1] (1986) study which reported that in 65.0 per cent of the cases, trade unions made the selection.

Criteria for Selection of Worker-Teacher

The Central Board for Workers' Education did not specify any qualifications or criteria for undergoing the training programmes of worker-teacher. CBWE rules say that "any industrial worker whether illiterate, trade union member or not and full time union official and staff should be eligible for the services provided by the board". Over the years, the unions generally nominate the workers for training and evolve their own criteria. One important criterion that has been followed by the union is the 'participation in union activities'. The unions while following the general criteria of active member of the union, also follow other criteria in the selection process. The workers' perception of the criteria followed by the union in nominating them for worker-teacher training were elicited and presented in the following table.

Table 5.2
Selection Criteria as Perceived by the Worker-Teachers

Criteria	*Frequency*	*Percentage*
Age	3	2.2
Education	33	24.6
Experience	39	29.1
Participation in trade union activities	59	44.1
Total	134	100.0

The data in the above table show that a large number (44.1%) of the workers felt that their active participation in union activities took them to the worker-teacher training and for about 29 per cent of workers the length of service in the organisation was reported to have been taken, followed by education (24.6%). It is generally said that the unions usually send workers who are very active in the union keeping in mind the necessity to develop future leadership and the same had been circulated among the workers. Virmani's (1986) also reported that nearly 43 per cent of the worker-teachers in his study felt that union participation is the main criterion for selection.

Motivators

Notwithstanding the fact that majority of the workers are nominated and sent by the organisation, to the training, there are a number of factors that motivate the workers to undergo training. People learn due to many and complex reasons. Motivation has been defined by David and Stephen P. Robins[4] (1989) as the willingness to do something and is conditioned by the action ability to satisfy some need for the individual.

A need according to them means some internal state that makes certain outcomes appear attractive. Some of the reasons for participation in learning are (1) they are sent, (2) they are asked to come, and (3) everyone is participating. Those nominated sometimes are *(a)* less productive and can be *(b)* easily spared *(c)* having the most seniority *(d)* have the least seniority. Those asked to come may have done so because *(i)* they want to learn *(ii)* want to get away from the job, *(iii)* feel it is a prestige assignment, *(iv)* think that everyone else is coming.

The reasons for undergoing worker-teacher training were probed and presented in the following table.

Table 5.3
Reasons for Undergoing Training

Reasons	*Frequency*	*Percentage*
To become trade union leader	25	18.7
To gain knowledge and imparting knowledge	85	63.4
To gain recognition	9	6.7
Due to union pressure	15	11.2
Total	134	100.0

An analysis of the factors that motivated the workers to undergo training, shows that majority (63.4%) of the respondents reported that they have undergone training to gain knowledge followed by 18.7 per cent of respondents who wanted to become leaders. It may be noticed from the table that around 11 per cent of the respondents come for the training because they were sent by the union. From the data it may be concluded that majority of the workers are motivated by the value of the training and other factors.

SECTION - B

Syllabus

Dictionary of Education[5] (1959) defined syllabus as the condensed outline or, statement of the main points of a course of study or of books or other documents. Any syllabus designed for training of workers must primarily be based on the aims and objectives of the scheme. The present syllabus for the worker-teachers and the unit level classes which has been the outcome of the recommendations of the Syllabus Review Committee aims to bring about many sided or all round development of the worker for the benefit of the country, his family and himself/herself (1982)[6].

As mentioned earlier, the Central Board for Workers' Education operates the programme in three tier.

1. Imparting of training to education officers.
2. On successful completion of training, the Education Officers are posted to different Regional Centres. They in turn impart training to selected workers-teachers.
3. The worker-teachers on completion of their training return to their establishments and conduct unit-level classes for the rank and file workers.

This section seeks to examine the views of the worker-teachers on the syllabus as it exists formally, its adequacy and the time allotted to cover the topics.

Know Your Country

The subject 'know your country' is divided into seven modules which dwell on historical aspects of the freedom struggle, socio-economic development of the country, cultural heritage, five-year plans, economic and geographical outlines

Table 5.4
Distribution of Respondents' Opinion on the Adequacy of Hours to Cover the Syllabus (Know Your Country)

No. of Hours	*Frequency*	*Percentage*
Less	31	23.1
Just right	40	29.9
More	63	47.0
Total	134	100.0

of the country. This chapter has been allotted 20 study units of one-hour duration. The respondents' views on this subject are analysed and given below.

An analysis of the responses to the above item in the syllabus 'know your country' to which 20 hours of teaching are allotted revealed that a large number (47.0%) of the respondents felt the time allotted to this item is more, and it does not require 20 hours of teaching. While a little over 23 per cent of the respondents said that the teaching hours allotted to it is inadequate, nearly 30% of them felt that the hours allotted to it are just right.

Know Your Country and Age

The data relating to the perceptions of the respondents towards the adequacy of hours for covering the above item and the ages of the respondents are presented in the following table.

Table 5.5

Distribution of Respondents' Opinion on the Adequacy of Hours to Cover the Syllabus (Know Your Country) and the Age

Age	*Less*	*Just Right*	*More*	*Total*
20 to 30 years	6 (18.2)	7 (21.2)	20 (60.6)	33 (24.6)
31 to 40 years	13 (17.8)	24 (32.9)	36 (49.3)	73 (54.5)
41 and above	12 (42.9)	9 (32.1)	7 (25.0)	28 (100.0)
Total	31	40	63	134

χ^2 = 11.31 d.f. 4; p<05

Analysis of the data on the adequacy of time to cover the item 'know your country' with the age of the respondents revealed that out of the respondents who are in the age group of 20 to 30 years, majority (60.6%) of them felt that the number of hours allotted to it (20 hours) is more and little over (18.2%) of them felt that the time is less, while about 21 per cent of them felt the time allotted to it is just right. In case of 31 to 40 years age group respondents, a large number (49.3%) of them considered the time allotted to it is high, almost 33 per cent of them felt 'just right', about 18 per cent felt it is less. In case of over 41 years of age cohort respondents, surprisingly, almost 43 per cent felt that the time allotted to it is less, about 32 per cent said 'just right' while one-fourth of them viewed it as less. From the table it is observed that the topic 'know your country' is not well received by younger respondents compared to middle aged respondents. The chi-square test revealed that there is an association between these two variables.

Know Your Country and Education

The following table shows the respondents perception towards the adequacy of time allotted for covering the topic 'know your country' and the 'education of respondents'.

Table 5.6
Distribution of Respondents' Opinion on the Adequacy of Hours to Cover the Syllabus (Know Your Country) and Education

Education	*Less*	*Just Right*	*More*	*Total*
Below SSC	14	10	19	43
	(32.6)	(23.3)	(44.1)	(32.1)
SSC	11	10	32	53
	(20.8)	(18.9)	(60.3)	(39.6)
Intermediate	1	7	8	16
	(6.3)	(43.7)	(50.0)	(11.9)
Degree	5	13	4	22
	(22.7)	(59.1)	(18.2)	(16.4)
Total	31	40	63	134
	(23.1)	(29.9)	(47.0)	(100.0)

χ^2 = 19.86; d.f. 4 p<05

The data in the table with regard to respondents'

educational attainments and their perception on the time allotted to cover the topic 'know your country', revealed that there is an association between education and the respondents' perception towards the above item. A large number of respondents (44%) with less than SSC qualification, majority (60.4%) of the SSC respondents and 50 per cent of the intermediate respondents found the time allotted to this item is 'more'. While majority (60.3%) of the respondents having degree qualification reported that the time allotted to it is 'just right'. From this table it is observed that respondents having degree qualification found the time allotted was just right. While others who have SSC and below education found the time allotted was more than required and felt that this time must be reduced. Less educated is less likely to favour teaching of subjects like know your country than better educated respondents.

Know Your Country and Type Job

The data relating to the perceptions of the respondents towards the adequacy of time allotted to cover the above item and their job are presented in the following table.

Table 5.7
Distribution of Respondents' Perceptions on the Adequacy of Hours to Cover the Syllabus (Know Your Country) and Type of Job

Job	*Less*	*Just Right*	*More*	*Total*
Technical	25 (24.3)	25 (23.3)	54 (52.4)	103 (76.9)
Non-technical	6 (19.4)	16 (51.6)	9 (29.0)	31 (23.1)
Total	31 (23.1)	40 (29.9)	63 (47.0)	134 (100.0)

χ^2 = 9.42; d.f. 4; p<05

An analysis of the data in the above table on the type of job and the respondents' perceptions on 'know your country', revealed that out of nearly 77 per cent of the technical job holders majority (52.4%) perceived that the time allotted to it was 'more'. A little over 24 per cent considered the time as less, and the rest felt the time allotted was 'just right'. In case of non-technical job holders, majority (51.6%) of them perceived the time allotted was just right, while 29 per cent favoured reduction of time for this item and the remaining respondents felt the time allotted was less. From this it is observed that technical job-holders are less likely to favour this item in the syllabus than the non-technical job-holders.

Virmani[7] (1986) in his study referring to course content 'know your country' observed that about two out of three months of the total training programme of worker-teachers is spent, dwelling on the glorious past of the country without proper discussion on the present day problems faced by the country. And the same is reflected in the perceptions of the worker-teachers. In the present study some respondents felt that this topic should be omitted from the course and other relevant topics may be included in the time allotted.

Know Your Industry

'Know Your Industry' is divided into seven modules which cover the topics like labour, capital in national development, industrial policy, modernisation and automation, industrial development five-year plans, industrial health and hygiene. 'Know your industry' is allotted eight hours. The responses were analysed and an overwhelming majority of the respondents (90.0%) expressed that the time allotted is more. Only 10 per cent said the time allotted is just right.

Productivity

It is spread over five modules and includes topics like meaning and concept of productivity, various aspects of productivity and role of public/private sector managements in increasing productivity. The chapter 'productivity education' is allotted 15 hours. The opinions of the respondents in this regard are presented in the following table.

Table 5.8
Distribution of Respondents' Opinion on the Adequacy of Hours Allotted to Cover Productivity

No. of Hours Allotted	*Frequency*	*Percentage*
Less	25	18.6
Just right	38	28.4
More	71	53.0
Total	134	100.0

From this table it can be noted that a majority of (53%) the respondents felt that the teaching hours allotted to it are very high, while nearly 19 per cent of them felt that the hours allotted are less. And the remaining (29%) felt that the hours allotted are just right.

From the table it is revealed that productivity education has not been well received by the worker-teachers as it is seen as management oriented subject. In fact managements in general insist on increased productivity whenever workers demand bonus and other incentives.

Productivity and Age

The data relating to the respondents opinion towards the time allotted for the item productivity and their ages are presented in the following table.

Analysis of the data on productivity by age of the respondents revealed that there is an association between these two variables namely, respondents' education and their perception towards productivity education. Out of the respondents who are in the age group of 20 to 30 years, majority of them (63.6%) felt the time allotted to it was 'more' while a little over 21 per cent said 'less' to this question and the remaining replied 'just right'. Similar trend is also observed in case of respondents who are in the age group of 41 years and above as an overwhelming majority (75.0%) of them found the time allotted was more. In case of respondents who are in the age group of 31 to 40 years, nearly 40 per cent of them felt the time allotted was just

Table 5.9
Distribution of Respondents Opinion on the Adequacy of Hours Allotted to Cover Productivity by Age

Age	*Less*	*Just Right*	*More*	*Total*
Below 30 years	7	5	21	33
	(21.2)	(15.2)	(63.6)	(24.6)
31 to 40 years	15	29	29	73
	(20.4)	(39.8)	(39.8)	(54.5)
41 and above	3	4	21	28
	(10.7)	(14.3)	(75.0)	(20.9)
Total	25	38	71	134
	(18.6)	(28.4)	(53.0)	(100.0)

χ^2 = 14.20364; d.f. 4; $p<0.05$

right, and 20.4 per cent opined the time allotted was less. The remaining, nearly 40 per cent favoured reduction in the time allotted to this item. From this table it is observed that lower age and higher age respondents are not well disposed towards productivity education, compared to middle aged group of 31 to 40 years respondents.

Industrial Relations

Industrial relations is divided into six chapters dealing with Labour Administration, mechanism for collective bargaining, code of discipline, grievance procedure, strike and lockout, importance of reducing man-days lost, need for avoidance of violence in trade union movement.

Table 5.10
Distribution of Respondents' Opinion on the Adequacy of Time Allotted to Cover Industrial Relations

No. of Hours Allotted	*Frequency*	*Percentage*
Less	50	37.3
Just right	51	38.1
More	33	24.6
Total	134	100.0

'Industrial Relations' is allotted 11 hours. The opinions of the respondents to this item were analysed and presented below.

It is observed from the above table that a little over 38 per cent of the respondents felt that the time allotted to it is just right while 37 per cent felt that the time allotted is less. And the remaining 25 per cent felt that the teaching time for this is high.

Trade Union Movement

Trade Union Movement is divided into 13 parts (20 hours) dealing with the history of national, international trade union movement, Gandhian Philosophy, its contributions to trade union movement. Trade union administration, organisation structure, finances, recognition of trade unions, drafting of charter of demands, dynamics of leadership, national and international federations of trade unions, social responsibility of workers four-fold obligations (1) to the country, (2) to the industry, (3) to the family, and (4) to trade unions from the content of trade union movement.

Table 5.11
Distribution of Respondents' Perceptions on the Adequacy of Time Allotted to Cover Trade Union Movement

Time Allotted	*Frequency*	*Percentage*
Less	25	18.7
Just right	40	29.8
More	69	51.5
Total	134	100.0

Majority of the respondents (51.5%) were of the view that the hours allotted to trade union movement are more. While nearly 30 per cent of them stated that hours allotted to it just right and around 19 per cent of them felt that teaching hours allotted to it is less.

A thorough probe into the responses revealed that under this item the past history of the trade union movement used to be discussed, according less attention to the present day union structure and functions. Holmstrom[8] (1985) opined that each union of workers has its distinct style, reflecting the idea of the people who nurtured it. The industrial workers may be less inclined towards histories and ideologies of unions, but more towards their mundane bread and butter problems.

Labour Economics

Labour economics has seven modules dealing mainly with concept of wages, minimum needs, dearness allowance, bonus, cost of living index and consumer price index, GNP/per capita income, their limitations and relative growth.

The chapter on labour economics is allotted 16 hours. The opinions of the respondents were analysed and presented below.

Table 5.12
Distribution of Respondents' Opinion of the Adequacy of Time Allotted to Cover 'Labour Economics'

No. of Hours Allotted	*Frequency*	*Percentage*
Less	57	42.6
Just right	44	32.8
More	33	24.6
Total	134	100.0

The responses to this item revealed that a large number (42.6%) of the respondents opined that time allotted to this item is less as it is the topic of their interest and they want more discussion or deliberations on this subject. About 33 per cent of them expressed that the teaching hours allotted to it is right, while nearly 25 per cent of them wanted reduction in the time. Some articulated workers would like to have discussions on liberalisation policies of the government and their impact on workers living standards.

Education for Participative Management

Education for participative management covers the topics like philosophy and concept of workers participation in industry, Gandhian theory of Trusteeship, functions of joint councils, effective participation in committee meetings.

Table 5.13
Distribution of Respondents' Perceptions on the Adequacy of Time Allotted to Education for Participative Management

Time Allotted	*Frequency*	*Percentage*
Less	76	56.7
Just right	37	27.6
More	21	15.7
Total	134	100.0

An analysis of the perceptions on the time allotted to the item "workers' participation in management", shows that majority (56.7%) of the workers perceived that the teaching hours allotted are less as it is the topic dear to the hearts of the workers. While about 28 per cent of the workers felt that the time allotted is just right, nearly 16 per cent of the workers felt that the time allotted is more than required for the topic. Workers' unions insist on participation at all levels of the industry which include the policies of management with regard to work guarantees for which the management may be unwilling or to agree to adopt an evasive approach.

Public Sector

Public sector and its role in the economy are divided into five modules. The chapter includes discussion on the origin and role of public sector, workers' participation in management in the public sector, perception of trade unions in the public sector, and importance and responsibilities of public, private and co-operative sectors. This has been allotted

18 sessions. The views of the respondents on this item are given below.

Table 5.14
Distribution of Respondents' Perceptions on Adequacy of Time Allotted to 'Public Sector'

Time Allotted	*Frequency*	*Percentage*
Less	18	13.4
Just right	42	31.3
More	74	55.3
Total	134	100.0

Data revealed that nearly one-third (31.3%) of the respondents opined that the hours allotted to this item are just right. While a majority (55.3%) of respondents felt it needs to be lessened, and the remaining (13.4%) respondents felt that there must be an increase in the number of hours. As it is the only sector which provides maximum employment and job security to the workers, and the fact that 80.0 per cent of the sample belong to public sector workers, it is surprising to note that they wanted reduction in the number of hours allotted to it. Being familiar with the industrial activity in this sphere, they may think that the less said the better.

Population Education and Family Welfare

It has five modules. It covers the topics like fertility, and other demographic aspects in relaticn to the national development, family welfare planning, personal hygiene and family budget. It has been allotted 13 hours. The responses to this item are given below.

An analysis of the perceptions on the time allotted to this item revealed that majority of the worker-teachers felt that the time allotted is more, while about 20 per cent opined that 11 sessions for this item is less and the remaining (24.6%) felt that the hours allotted are 'just right'.

Table 5.15
Distribution of Respondents' Perceptions on the Adequacy of Time Allotted to 'Population Education and Family Welfare'

Perception	*Frequency*	*Percentage*
Less	27	20.1
Just right	33	24.6
More	74	55.3
Total	134	100.0

Labour Legislation

This is divided into three modules. First module deals with Labour Legislation and Administration and it is allotted one study unit. Second module is divided into four chapters covering important wage legislation, Industrial Relations Legislation, Social Security Legislation and Welfare Legislation. The third module covers important state labour acts.

Table 5.16
Distribution of Respondents' Perception on the Item 'Labour Laws'

Perception	*Frequency*	*Percentage*
Less	99	73.9
Just right	15	11.1
More	20	15.0
Total	134	100.0

An analysis of responses to this item revealed that an overwhelming majority of the respondents (73.9%) are of the view that the time allotted to this item is less, while about 11 per cent of them said that the time allotted to it is just right. Only 15 per cent of them perceived that the time allotted is more. In the opinion of workers, knowledge of labour laws helps the workers in the assertion of their rights vis-a-vis the management. Knowledge of law is important from the workers point of view, as such given laws tilted in favour of workers and they are instruments through which workers protect themselves.

Worker-teachers were of the view that the trainers were not well informed about the labour laws and social legislations. None of the acts listed in the syllabus was taught in the worker-teacher training. They felt as these acts were of more relevance and useful and legal experts should handle them.

Communication Techniques

The communication techniques practicals which have been allotted 91 hours in the syllabus are divided into 14 modules or sections. It covers the topics like methods of persuasion, nature of learning process, moderating group discussions, seminars, importance of audio-visual aids, motivation, practical use of audio-visual aids, teaching practice and field visits.

Theoretical part of the methods of communication is allotted 20 hours. Under practicals, accounted for 37 hours, field visits and examinations accounted for 25 and 10 hours respectively. The responses to this item are presented below.

Table 5.17
Distribution of Respondents' Opinion on 'Communication Techniques'

Perception	*Frequency*	*Percentage*
Less	12	9.0
Just right	54	40.3
More	68	50.7
Total	134	100.0

An analysis of responses to this item revealed that a majority (50.7%) of them opined that the time allotted to it is more. While a little over 40 per cent said that the time allotted is just right and the remaining (9.0%) respondents reported that the time allotted to it is less. Under this item a majority of workers find topics like learning process, motivation etc. as too obtuse for easy comprehension, hence their negative perception towards all aspects of communication techniques.

Summary

An analysis of the responses to the curriculum and the time allotted to them in the training programme suggests that topics like know your country, public sector, productivity, trade union movement and communication techniques were not favoured by worker-teachers. They felt that time allotted to these topics needs to be curtailed and an overwhelming majority of the respondents favoured hike in the number of hours allotted to labour legislation and some workers suggested inclusion of civil and criminal laws in the syllabus.

Techniques of communication, an important topic helpful to them in discharging their teachers' duties, which is accorded one-third of the time, has not been well received by the respondents. This may be due to the over emphasis given to the theoretical aspects neglecting the need to train the workers in the teaching techniques. It is needless to say training them in the practical aspects help to become good teachers.

SECTION - C

Training

This section seeks to examine the views of the worker-teachers on the various facets of training they received at the regional centre. The duration of training, coverage of the syllabus, training methodology, quantity and quality of training material, level of inputs and the involvement of the trainee in the programme are the variables that have been used as parameters for assessing the adequacy of the training programme.

Duration of Training

The period of training programme is a very important factor influencing the learning process of the trainee. Timing of the programme must be realistic and flexible. Realistic because the trainee needs sufficient time to learn and be flexible because trainees vary in the speed at which they learn, instructors vary in the speed at which they promote the learning and the conditions under which learning takes place vary from day to day (ILO, 1985)[9].

The workers' education programme envisaged a three-month full time worker-teacher training course. During this period the syllabus or course content discussed in the preceding pages to be imparted to the trainees. The present study elicited the perceptions of the workers teachers on the adequacy of the duration of training of worker-teacher and opinions of the respondents are presented below.

Table 5.18
Distribution of Respondents Perception on the Duration of Training

Responses	*Frequency*	*Percentage*
Less	72	53.7
Just right	44	32.8
More	18	13.5
Total	134	100.0

A majority (53.7%) of the respondents felt that the present period of training is not sufficient and must be extended, while nearly one-third of the workers opined that the present period of training is sufficient, and the remaining (13.5%) the respondents felt that period of training is too long and it must be reduced.

Age and Duration of Training

An analysis of the data revealed that out of nearly one-fourth of the respondents in the age group of 20 to 30 years, a majority (75.8%) of them felt that the duration is less. About 21 per cent said that the duration is just right followed by three per cent of them who considered the present duration more than sufficient. Out of the 54.5 per cent of the respondents who fall in the age cohort of 31 to 40 years, nearly 41 per cent of them felt that the programme duration is less, followed by an equal number of them who said that the duration is just right. The remaining (17.8%) respondents felt that the duration is more. Out of the respondents who belonged to the age group of 41 years and above, a majority of them (60.7%) felt that the duration is less, followed by 25 per cent who felt that the duration is just right. The remaining (14.3%) felt that the duration is a prolonged one. From the data it is noticed that majority of young worker-teacher found the duration less, compared to the middle aged workers.

Table 5.19
Distribution of Respondents Opinion on the Duration of Training and Age

Age group	*Less*	*Just Right*	*More*	*Total*
20 to 30 years	25 (75.8)	7 (21.2)	1 (3.0)	33 (24.6)
31 to 40 years	30 (41.1)	30 (41.1)	13 (17.8)	73 (54.5)
41 & above	17 (60.7)	7 (25.0)	4 (14.3)	28 (20.9)
Total	72 (53.7)	44 (32.8)	18 (13.5)	134 (100.0)

χ^2 = 12.51509; d.f. 4 p<.05

The chi-square test reveals a significant association between the two attributes, namely, respondents' age and their perception towards the duration of training period as the calculated value of χ^2 is 12.5, which is significant at five per cent level.

Job and Duration of Training

An analysis of the data revealed that out of the respondents whose nature of job is technical, a majority (61.2%) of them felt that the period is not sufficient, while nearly one-third (31.1%) of them felt that the duration is just right. The remaining 7.8 per cent were of the view that the programme duration is lengthy. Out of the 23.1 per cent of the non-technical respondents 29 per cent of them felt that the programme duration is short, followed by almost 39 per cent of respondents who felt that the duration is just right. The remaining (32.3%) respondents felt that the duration is more. The respondents holding technical jobs find the programme interesting as they are not well versed with subject matter of the programme and the present duration of 3 months period was seen too short by them. The respondents with white-collar jobs and well versed with the subject matter of the programme felt that the duration is just sufficient. This opinion is due to their nature of job.

Table 5.20
Distribution of Respondents Opinion on the Duration of Training the Nature of Job

Job	*Less*	*Just Right*	*More*	*Total*
Technical	63 (61.2)	32 (31.1)	8 (7.8)	103 (76.9)
Non-technical	9 (29.0)	12 (38.7)	10 (32.3)	11 (23.1)
Total	72 (53.7)	44 (32.8)	18 (13.5)	134 (100.0)

χ^2 = 15.64270; d.f. 4 p<.05

Duration of Training and Education

Analysis of data relating to period of training and respondents' education revealed that out of the respondents whose educational background is below Secondary School Certificate an overwhelming majority (76.8%) of them opined that the present period of training is not sufficient, while nearly 12 per cent of them felt it is just right, and an equal percentage of them felt that the training period is lengthier than normal. Out of the respondents who have SSC qualification, majority (58.5%) of them felt that the duration of the programme is too short to cover the syllabus while nearly one-third of them felt that the present time is sufficient. The remaining (7.5%) of them felt that the present period is long. Out of the respondents who have intermediate qualification, a majority (68.7%) of them felt that duration is just right. In case of the respondents who have Bachelors Degree qualification, a large number (45.5%) of them felt that the duration is just right, while nearly 14 per cent of them opined that the period is not sufficient, almost 41 per cent of them felt that the period of training is longer.

Table 5.21
Education and Perceptions Towards Period of Training

Education	*Less*	*Just Right*	*More*	*Total*
Below SSC	33 (76.8)	5 (11.6)	5 (11.6)	43 (32.1)
SSC	31 (58.5)	18 (34.0)	4 (7.5)	53 (39.6)
Intermediate	5 (31.3)	18 (68.81)	—	16 (11.9)
Degree	3 (13.6)	10 (45.5)	9 (40.9)	22 (16.4)
Total	72 (53.7)	44 (32.8)	18 (13.4)	134 (100.0)

χ^2 = 41.79585; d.f. 4 p<.05

From this table it can be seen that the less educated respondents felt that the duration of training programme was not adequate and more educated have opined that the time is sufficient.

Duration of Training and Experience

An analysis of the data revealed that out of the respondents who have an experience of eight years and below a majority (65.8%) of them opined that the duration is not sufficient, while about 29 per cent of them felt that the duration is just right. The remaining (5.3 per cent) respondents said that the duration is longer. Out of the respondents who have an experience of 9 to 16 years, nearly 43 per cent of them opined that the duration is not sufficient, and about 37 per cent of them felt that the duration is quite sufficient. For the remaining (20.6%) respondents the duration is more. In case of respondents who have above 17 years of experience, a majority (60.6%) of them felt that the duration of training is less, 30 per cent felt that it is sufficient, while a little over nine per cent of them opined that the duration is longer. From this table it can be seen that the majority of respondents in all categories found the duration of the programme insufficient. From this it can be concluded that level of experience has no bearing on the perception towards duration of the training programme.

Table 5.22
Respondents' Perception Towards Period of Training and Experience

Experience	*Less*	*Just Right*	*More*	*Total*
0 to 8 years	25 (65.8)	11 (28.9)	2 (5.3)	38 (28.4)
9 to 16 years	27 (42.9)	23 (36.5)	13 (20.6)	63 (47.0)
17 & above	20 (60.6)	10 (30.3)	3 (9.1)	33 (24.6)
Total	72 (53.7)	44 (32.8)	18 (13.4)	134 (100.0)

$\chi^2 = 7.9$; d.f. 4 $p>.05$

Coverage of the Syllabus

Coverage of the syllabus is more important than that of the syllabus itself. Coverage of the syllabus depends to a large extent on the duration of the course, and the trainers knowledge base. It is important that the subjects of the programme are covered in a pattern, that sustains the interest of the trainee to learn. There are three ways of covering the syllabus (ILO[10], 1985).

1. The whole of the syllabus to be learned is first covered in broad outline and then each item or subject is dealt in an in-depth manner.
2. The whole of the syllabus or material to be learned may be covered in several stages/times over, increasing the depth each time.
3. Each item or subject may be presented separately and the 'parts' brought into a 'whole' at the end of the programme.

The worker-teachers views on the coverage of the course content were elicited and presented in the following table.

Table 5.23
Distribution of Worker-Teachers Perceptions Regarding Coverage of Syllabus

Perceptions	*Frequency*	*Percentage*
Poor	51	38.1
Good	42	31.3
Outstanding	41	30.6
Total	134	100.0

Regarding coverage of the syllabus a large number (38.1%) of the workers felt that the coverage of the topics was poor. A little over 31 per cent of them felt that the coverage was good and the remaining (30.6%) opined that it was outstanding.

Coverage and Age

An analysis of the data in the table revealed that out of 24.6 per cent of the respondent who are below 30 years of age a large number of them (42.5%) found the coverage outstanding. Out of the 54.5 pe rcent of the respondents who are in the 31 to 40 years of age, almost 40 per cent of them felt that the coverage of syllabus was poor, while 26 per cent of them felt that the coverage was outstanding. The remaining 34.2 per cent of them found the coverage good. In case of respondents who are in the age group of 41 and above 33.3 per cent of them felt that the coverage is poor, while nearly 29 per cent of them felt that the coverage is outstanding.

Table 5.24
Distribution of Respondents Opinion on Coverage and Age

Age	*Poor*	*Good*	*Outstanding*	*Total*
20 to 30 years	11 (33.3)	8 (24.2)	14 (42.5)	33 (24.6)
31 to 40 years	29 (39.7)	25 (34.3)	19 (26.0)	73 (54.5)
41 & above	11 (33.3)	9 (32.1)	8 (28.6)	28 (20.9)
Total	51 (38.1)	42 (31.3)	41 (30.6)	134 (100.0)

Coverage of Syllabus and Education

An analysis of the data relating to the educational qualifications of the respondents and their perception towards coverage of the syllabus revealed that out of those who have below SSC education, a large number (37.2%) perceived that the coverage was outstanding. In case of those who have SSC qualification, two-fifths (39.7%) felt that the coverage was outstanding. About 44 per cent of the intermediate background felt that the coverage was poor. In case of the respondents with Bachelor degree and above an overwhelming majority (86.4%) perceived coverage as poor. From the data it can be inferred that higher educated are perceiving the coverage as poor compared to others.

Table 5.25
Level of Education and Coverage of the Syllabus

Education	*Poor*	*Good*	*Outstanding*	*Total*
Below SSC	12 (27.9)	15 (34.9)	16 (37.2)	43 (32.1)
SSC	13 (24.5)	19 (35.8)	21 (39.6)	53 (39.6)
Intermediate	7 (43.8)	6 (37.5)	3 (18.8)	16 (11.9)
Degree	19 (86.4)	2 (9.1)	1 (4.5)	22 (16.4)
Total	51 (86.4)	42 (31.3)	41 (30.6)	134 (100.0)

χ^2 = 29.16140; d.f. 4 p<.05

Coverage and Type of Job

The data relating to the type of job and the respondents' perceptions towards coverage of the syllabus during their training period, revealed that nearly thirty-seven per cent of the respondents who hold technical jobs perceived the coverage as outstanding while 67 per cent of the non-technical job holders rated it as poor.

Table 5.26
Type of Job and Coverage

Type of Job	*Poor*	*Good*	*Outstanding*	*Total*
Technical	30 (29.1)	35 (34.0)	38 (36.9)	103 (76.9)
Non-technical	21 (67.7)	7 (22.7)	3 (9.7)	31 (23.1)
Total	51 (38.1)	42 (31.3)	41 (30.6)	134 (100.0)

χ^2 = 16.0923; d.f. 4 p<.05

From this table it can be observed that the non-technical

job holders, *i.e.*, white collar workers, with their relatively higher educational background, have low opinion with regard to the coverage of the topics in the syllabus. The fact that 67 per cent of the white collar workers have rated the coverage as poor compared to nearly 29 per cent of blue collar workers who rated the coverage as poor indicate that the programme has no takers in the white collar category workers.

Level of Inputs

A training programme, which covers the right items or subjects, may fail to achieve its objectives if it is pitched at the wrong level. The level of inputs must be matched with the trainees abilities. When the material to be learned is of high level, the average trainee will be unable to learn. When the material to be learned is of low level, trainee often rejects the whole of the programme. That is why the question of 'level' needs to be carefully assessed (ILO, 1985)[11].

Table 5.27
Distribution of Worker-Teachers Perceptions Regarding The Level of Inputs in the Training Programme

Opinion	*Frequency*	*Percentage*
Advance	59	44.0
Just Right	49	36.6
Elementary	26	19.4
Total	134	100.0

Regarding the level of inputs in the training programme a large number (44%) of the workers felt it is too advanced to follow, and around 19 per cent of the respondents felt that it is too elementary and only 37 per cent felt that the level of inputs is just right.

Level of Inputs and Age

An analysis of the data revealed that out of the respondents who are in the age group of 20 to 30 a majority (66.7%) of them stated that the level of inputs is advanced. In case of the respondents who are in the age group of 31 to 40 a large number of them (38%) opined the level of inputs as high. With regard to the respondents who are above 41 years a majority (57.1%) of them expressed satisfaction with the level of inputs. From this table it is observed that the higher age group respondents are rating the level of inputs as just right compared to young workers who might not be capable enough to comprehend the intricacies of the subject. It is also found that the two attributes namely respondents' age and their perception towards level of inputs are significantly associated after applying chi-square test.

Table 5.28
Distribution of Worker-Teachers Perceptions Regarding the Level of Inputs and Age

Age	*Advance*	*Just Right*	*Elementary*	*Total*
20 to 30 years	22 (66.7)	7 (21.2)	4 (12.1)	33 (24.6)
31 to 40 years	28 (38.4)	26 (35.6)	19 (26.0)	73 (54.5)
41 & above	9 (32.1)	16 (57.1)	3 (10.7)	28 (20.9)
Total	59 (44.0)	49 (36.6)	26 (19.4)	134 (100.0)

χ^2 = 14.302; d.f. 4 p<.05

Level of Inputs and Education

An analysis of the data relating to the respondents' education and their perceptions towards level of inputs, shows that out of the respondents who have below SSC education, a majority (60.5 per cent) rated the level of inputs as high or advanced. Out of the respondents who have SSC level, majority (56.6%) rated the level of inputs as advanced, while 34.0 per cent of them felt the level as just right.

In case of respondents who have intermediate

qualification majority (68.8%) told that the level of inputs were just right, 12.5 per cent of them found the level of inputs as advance while nearly 19 per cent of them felt that the level of inputs is elementary. Out of the respondents who have degree qualification, majority (54.5%) viewed the level of inputs as elementary. From this table it is observed that less educated respondents found the level of inputs as 'advanced', while respondents with higher educational background found the inputs as elementary. It is also found that the two variables namely respondents' education and their perceptions towards level of inputs are significantly associated.

Table 5.29

Level of Education and Level of Inputs

Education	*Advance*	*Just Right*	*Elementary*	*Total*
Below SSC	26	11	6	43
	(60.5)	(25.5)	(14.0)	(32.1)
SSC	30	18	5	53
	(56.6)	(34.0)	(9.4)	(39.6)
Intermediate	2	11	93	16
	(12.5)	(68.7)	(18.8)	(11.9)
Degree	1	9	12	22
	(4.5)	(41.0)	(54.5)	(16.4)
Total	59	49	26	134
	(44.0)	(36.6)	(19.4)	(100.0)

χ^2 = 39.4854; d.f. 4 p<.05

Level of Inputs and Type of Job

In order to examine effect of respondents' nature of job and their perceptions towards the level of inputs, two variables were cross-tabulated and presented in the following table.

It can be seen from the table that out of the respondents who hold technical jobs, a majority, (51.5%) felt that the level of inputs are high or advanced, while nearly 37 per cent said they are just right. Out of the white-collar worker-teacher respondents, a little over 45 per cent of them felt that the inputs are elementary, while 35.5 per cent said that they are optimum.

Table 5.30
Distribution of Respondents Perceptions Regarding Level of Inputs and the Type of Job

Type of Job	*Advance*	*Just Right*	*Elementary*	*Total*
Technical	53	38	12	103
	(51.5)	(36.9)	(11.7)	(76.9)
Non-technical	6	11	4	31
	(19.4)	(35.5)	(45.2)	(23.1)
Total	59	49	26	134
	(44.0)	(36.6)	(19.4)	(100.0)

χ^2 = 19.38; d.f. 4; $p<.05$

Level of Inputs and Experience

The data relating to the respondents perception towards level of input and their experience levels were cross-tabulated and are presented in the following table.

Table 5.31
Distribution of Respondents' Perception Regarding the Level of Inputs and Experience

Experience	*Advance*	*Just Right*	*Elementary*	*Total*
Below 8 years	20	9	9	38
	(52.6)	(23.7)	(23.7)	(28.4)
9 to 16 years	27	25	11	63
	(42.8)	(39.7)	(17.5)	(47.0)
17 & years	12	15	6	33
	(36.4)	(45.5)	(18.2)	(24.6)
Total	59	49	26	134
	(44.0)	(36.6)	(19.4)	(100.0)

An analysis of the data revealed that among the

respondents who have below eight years of experience, a majority of them (52.6%) felt that the level of inputs are advanced, as against 23.7 per cent of the respondents who felt that the inputs are just right or satisfactory. The remaining felt that they are too elementary. In case of the respondents who are in the age group of 9 to 16 years a large number of them (42.0%) felt that the levels of inputs are advanced, while nearly 40 per cent of them felt that they are satisfactory and for the remaining (17.5%) respondents the level of inputs is elementary. In case of respondents who are having an experience of 17 years and above, a large number (45.5%) of them felt that the level of inputs is just right while thirty-six per cent felt that level of inputs is high as against nearly 18 per cent who rated the level of inputs as elementary.

Training Methodology

The training methodology has a bearing on the process of learning. The methods of training or teaching must respect the *(a)* intellectual level and educational background of the participants, *(b)* the participants' age and practical experience, and *(c)* the social and external environment (Kubr, M., 1985)[12]. The workers' education programme envisaged the use of the following methods of teaching for its worker-teachers training programme like lecture, seminar, role play, conference, case study method and workshop. The perceptions of the workers on the type of methodology used are presented in the following table.

Table 5.32
Distribution of Worker-Teachers' Perceptions About Training Methodology

Training	*Frequency*	*Percentage*
Poor	74	55.2
Good	32	23.9
Outstanding	28	20.9
Total	134	100.0

An analysis of the perceptions of the worker teacher about training methodology adopted in the training programme, shows that a majority (55.2%) of the respondents felt that the training methodology (teaching aids, etc.) used in the training programme is poor.

Age and Training Methodology

An analysis of the data in the table revealed that among the respondents who are in the age group of 20 to 30, a large number (42.4%) have rated the training methodology as poor. While majority (63.0%) of the respondents belonging to 31 to 40 years age group and above 41 years respondents (50.0%) also perceived the programme as poor. From this table it can be seen that majority of the respondents in all the age groups have perceived similarly regarding the training methodology. There is no more variation with regard to their perceptions towards training methodology among different age groups of respondents. The chi-square test also revealed that there is no association between these two variables.

Table 5.33
Age and Training Methodology

Age	*Poor*	*Good*	*Very Good*	*Total*
20 to 30 years	14	11	8	33
	(42.4)	(33.3)	(24.2)	(24.6)
31 to 40 years	46	14	13	73
(63.0)	(19.2)	(17.8)	(54.5)	
41 & above	14	7	7	28
	(50.0)	(25.0)	(25.0)	(20.9)
Total	74	32	28	134
	(55.2)	(23.9)	(20.9)	(100.0)

χ^2 = 4.58059; d.f. 4>.05

Education and Training Methodology

From the association of the respondents' educational attainments with their perceptions towards training methodology, it is noticed that out of the respondents who have below SSC qualification nearly 40 per cent stated that the training methodology was poor. Out of the respondents who have SSC qualification, a large majority (73.6%) rated the training methodology as poor. In case of respondents having intermediate qualification a large number (37.5%) found it good and another 37.5 per cent found it very good. In case of respondents having degree qualification a majority (63.6%) of them rated it as poor.

Table 5.34
Distribution of Respondents Perception Regarding the Training Methodology and Age

Education	*Poor*	*Good*	*Very Good*	*Total*
Below SSC	17	13	13	43
	(39.5)	(30.2)	(30.2)	(32.1)
SSC	39	10	4	53
	(73.6)	(18.9)	(7.5)	(39.6)
Intermediate	4	6	6	16
	(25.0)	(37.5)	(37.5)	(11.9)
Degree	14	3	5	22
	(63.6)	(13.6)	(22.7)	(16.4)
Total	74	32	28	134
	(55.2)	(23.9)	(20.9)	(100.0)

χ^2 = 20.03429; d.f. 6 p<.05

From the table it is observed that the respondents having degree qualification have how level of opinion about the training methodology, compared to the respondents with below SSC and intermediate qualification.

Type of Job and Training Methodology

An analysis of the data revealed that there is no association between these two variables namely, type of job and training methodology. From this table it is observed that in both the categories of jobs, a majority of them rated the training methodology as poor.

Table 5.35
Distribution of Respondents Perception Regarding the Training Methodology and Education

Job	*Poor*	*Good*	*Very Good*	*Total*
Technical	46 (54.4)	26 (25.2)	21 (20.4)	103 (76.9)
Non-technical	18 (58.1)	2 (19.4)	7 (22.6)	31 (23.1)
Total	74 (55.2)	32 (23.9)	28 (20.9)	134 (100.0)

χ^2 = 0.45965; d.f. = 2; p>0.05

Experience and Training Methodology

An analysis of the data revealed that respondents who are in the age group of below eight years of experience, a large number (47.4%) has poor opinion about the training methodology. Among the respondents having 9 to 16 years of experience, majority (60.3%) rated the training methodology as poor. Among the respondents having 17 years and above experience majority (55.0%) had rated the training methodology as poor. From this table it is observed, in all categories, majority of the respondents rated the training methodology as poor.

Table 5.36
Distribution of Respondents Perception Regarding Experience and Training Methodology

Experience	*Poor*	*Good*	*Very Good*	*Total*
Below 8 years	18 (47.4)	10 (26.3)	10 (26.3)	38 (28.4)
9 to 16 years	38 (60.3)	14 (22.2)	11 (17.5)	63 (47.0)
17 & above	18 (54.5)	8 (24.2)	7 (21.2)	33 (24.6)
Total	74 (55.2)	32 (23.9)	28 (20.9)	134 (100.0)

χ^2 = 1.7837; d.f. = 4; p<0.05

Our interviews with the worker-teachers revealed that lecture method was given prominence and other methods of teaching like role-play, seminar, were not at all used. Sometimes discussion method was allowed. Use of audio-visual aids in the training programme was also minimal.

Material (Quantity)

The views of the worker-teachers on the quantity and quality of material are presented in the following tables.

Adequate care should be taken to ensure the relevance and suitability of training material and also the method of presentation of the subject in question. Most of the instructor's time that is spent in speech may be saved if appropriate written material is available to the trainee for study (ILO[13], 1985).

Table 5.37
Distribution of Worker-Teachers Perceptions Regarding The Reading Material Supplied

Perceptions	*Frequency*	*Percentage*
Less	33	24.6
Just Right	44	32.9
More	57	42.5
Total	134	100.0

Regarding the reading material supplied by the board during the training programme, a large number (42.5%) of respondents perceived the material supplied by them is more than sufficient. Nearly 33 per cent of the respondents felt that the material is just right, while about 25 per cent of them felt that the material supplied by them is not up to the mark.

Quantity of the Training Material and the Age

The data relating to the perceptions of the respondents towards the training material (quantity) and their ages are presented in the following table.

Table 5.38
Distribution of Respondents Perception Towards Material and the Age

Age	*Less*	*Just Right*	*Much*	*Total*
20 to 30 years	6 (18.2)	14 (42.4)	13 (39.4)	33 (24.6)
31 to 40 years	18 (24.7)	19 (26.0)	36 (49.3)	73 (54.5)
41 & above	9 (32.1)	11 (39.3)	8 (28.6)	28 (20.9)
Total	33 (24.6)	44 (32.8)	57 (42.5)	134 (100.0)

$\chi^2 = 5.657$; d.f. = 4; $p<0.05$

An analysis of the data revealed that there is no association between these two variables *i.e.* age of the respondents and their perceptions towards quantity of training material. The table makes it clear that among the respondents in the age group of 20 to 30 years, about 42 per cent of them said it is just right. Only about 18 per cent of them were of the opinion that the quantity of the material supplied during the training programme was less. Similar trend is also observed among the respondents in the age groups of 31 to 40 years and of 41 years and above. The chi-square test also revealed that there is no association between the respondents' age and their perceptions towards training material.

Training Material and Education

The perception of the respondents towards training material and the level of education are presented in the following table.

An analysis of data with regard to the respondents' education and their perception towards quantity of training material revealed that there is no association between these two variables. It is observed that majority of the respondents in all categories of educational groups rated the reading material as much.

Table 5.39
Perceptions of Respondents Towards Training Material and Education

Education	*Less*	*Just Right*	*Much*	*Total*
Below SSC	16	12	15	43
	(37.2)	(27.9)	(34.9)	(32.1)
SSC	7	20	26	53
	(13.2)	(37.7)	(49.1)	(39.6)
Intermediate	3	4	9	16
	(18.8)	(25.0)	(56.3)	(11.9)
Degree	7	8	7	22
	(31.8)	(36.4)	(31.8)	(16.4)
Total	33	44	57	134
	(24.6)	(32.8)	(42.5)	(100.0)

χ^2 = 9.7685; d.f. = 6; p<0.05

Training Material and Experience

The data on the perceptions of the respondents towards training material and the level of experience is presented in the following table.

Table 5.40
Perceptions of the Respondents on the Quantity of Material and Experience

Experience	*Less*	*Just Right*	*Much*	*Total*
0 to 8 years	8	14	16	38
	(21.1)	(36.8)	(42.1)	(28.4)
9 to 16 years	13	19	31	63
	(20.6)	(30.2)	(49.2)	(47.0)
17 & above	12	11	10	33
	(36.4)	(33.3)	(30.3)	(24.6)
Total	33	44	57	134
	(24.6)	(32.8)	(42.5)	(100.0)

χ^2 = 4.597; d.f. = 4; p<0.05

The data in the table indicate that there is no association between the two variables namely experience and the respondents' perception towards quantity of training material. Out of the respondents having less than eight years of experience a large number (42.0%) perceived it as more. In case of respondents who are in the 9 to 16 years of age group nearly half of them (49.2%) felt the same. In case of respondents with more than 17 years a large number of them (30.3%) perceived it as less. The chi-square test revealed there is no association between these two variables.

Material Quality

The data on the perceptions of the respondents towards the quality of the training material are presented in the following table.

Table 5.41
Distribution of Worker-Teachers Perceptions Regarding The Quality of Material Supplied

Perceptions	*Frequency*	*Percentage*
Poor	38	28.4
Good	49	36.6
Outstanding	47	35.0
Total	134	100.0

Regarding the quality of material supplied to them, a large number of the respondents (36.6%) felt that the material is good. Only about 28 per cent of the respondents opined that the quality of the material is poor.

Quality of Training Material and Education

The data on the quality of the training and respondents education are presented in the following table.

An analysis of the data revealed that out of the respondents having below SSC educational qualifications, a large number of them (46.5%) perceived quality of material

Table 5.42
Education and Quality of Reading Material

Education	*Poor*	*Good*	*Outstanding*	*Total*
Below SSC	5 (11.6)	18 (41.9)	20 (46.5)	43 (32.1)
SSC	16 (30.2)	15 (28.3)	22 (41.5)	53 (39.6)
Intermediate	3 (18.8)	12 (75.0)	1 (6.3)	16 (11.9)
Degree	14 (63.6)	4 (18.2)	4 (18.2)	22 (16.4)
Total	38 (28.4)	49 (36.6)	47 (35.1)	134 (100.0)

χ^2 = 32.10839; d.f. = 6; $p<0.05$

as outstanding and similar trend is also observed in case of respondents with SSC qualifications. From the table it is observed that majority of the (63.6%) higher educated workers perceived the quality as poor. This shows that higher educated respondents have low opinion about the quality while less educated respondents perceived them as outstanding.

Quality of Training Material and Type of Job

The following table depicts the perceptions of the respondents towards quality of training and their nature of job.

Table 5.43
Distribution of Respondents Perception Towards Quality of Material and Type of Job

Job	*Poor*	*Good*	*Outstanding*	*Total*
Technical	22 (21.4)	39 (37.9)	42 (40.8)	103 (76.9)
Non-technical	16 (51.6)	10 (32.3)	5 (16.1)	31 (23.1)
Total	74 (55.2)	32 (23.9)	28 (20.9)	134 (100.0)

χ^2 = 12.02277; d.f. = 2; $p<0.05$

The data in the table show that a large number of technical jobholders perceived (40.8%) the quality as outstanding, while more than 50.0 per cent of the non-technical job holders perceived it as poor. It signifies that the nature of the job has a bearing on the perceptions of the respondents.

Quality of Material and Experience

The perceptions of the respondents on the quality of training material and their experience levels are presented in the following table.

Table 5.44
Distribution of Respondents Perception Towards Quality of Material and Experience

Experience	*Poor*	*Good*	*Outstanding*	*Total*
0 to 8 years	8	17	13	38
	(21.1)	(44.7)	(34.2)	(28.4)
9 to 16 years	23	21	19	63
	(36.5)	(33.3)	(30.2)	(47.0)
17 & above	7	11	15	33
	(21.2)	(33.3)	(45.5)	(24.6)
Total	38	32	28	134
	(55.2)	(23.9)	(20.9)	(100.0)

$\chi^2 = 5.20$; d.f. = 4; $p<0.05$

The results of the analysis of the data revealed that there is no association between the two variables namely respondents' experience and thier perception towards quality of material supplied to them. Out of the respondents who have below 8 years of experience a majority (79.0%) of them rated the materials quality as 'good' to 'outstanding', while 64.0 per cent of respondents with 9 to 16 years of experience and 79.0 per cent with above 17 years experience have also rated the quality of material good to outstanding.

Trainee Involvement

The principle of actual involvement is perhaps the main "raisond'etre" of the training programme. The greater the involvement, the higher the motivation, the more the participants retain the better and they are equipped to apply it. Involvement also depends on the leadership style, teaching method or the performance of the teacher (Kubr, 1985)[14].

The views of the worker-teachers on their involvement in the training programme are presented in the following tables.

Table 5.45
Distribution of Respondents Opinions Regarding Their Involvement in the Training Programme

Perception	*Frequency*	*Percentage*
Poor	61	45.5
Good	39	29.1
Outstanding	34	25.4
Total	134	100.0

Regarding the involvement of respondents in the training programme a large number (45.5%) of the respondents rated their involvement as poor, while 55.0 per cent of them rated it as 'good' to 'outstanding'.

Trainee Involvement and Age

The data on the perceptions of the respondents towards their involvement and their ages are presented in the following table.

An analysis of the data revealed that out of the respondents who are in the group of 20 to 30 years, majority (66.7%) rated their participation as poor. In case of respondents in the age group of 31-40 years, a large number of them (41.1%) rated it as poor. In the case of respondents with 41 and above age group a large number of them (35.7%) rated very good. From the table it is observed that

Table 5.46
Distribution of Respondents Perception Towards Their Involvement and Age

Age	*Poor*	*Good*	*Outstanding*	*Total*
20 to 30 years	22 (66.7)	6 (18.2)	5 (15.2)	33 (24.6)
31 to 40 years	30 (41.1)	24 (32.9)	19 (26.0)	73 (54.5)
41 & above	9 (32.1)	9 (32.1)	10 (35.7)	28 (20.9)
Total	61 (45.5)	39 (29.1)	34 (25.4)	134 (100.0)

χ^2 = 9.00600; d.f. 4; $p<0.05$

the respondents in the lower age group (20-30 years) had poor involvement while higher age group respondents had active involvement in the training programme. The application of chi-square test also revealed that there is an association between these two variables as the χ^2 = 9.006 is significant at 5% level.

Trainee Involvement and Education

Cross tabulating the data with the educational attainments of the respondents revealed that out of the respondents who have below SSC qualification, a large majority (58.1%) of them rated their involvement as poor. Out of the respondents with SSC qualifications a large majority (60.4%) considered their involvement as poor. In case of respondents with intermediate qualifications 50.0 per cent of them rated involvement as good. While a large majority (54.5%) of the respondents with degree and above qualification rated their involvement as very good.

From this table it is observed that the involvement of the trainee is dependent on the educational attainments of the respondents and the data in the table clearly proved it. The chi-square test also revealed that there is an association between these two variables.

Table 5.47
Distribution of Respondents Perception Regarding Involvement and Education

Education	*Poor*	*Good*	*Outstanding*	*Total*
Below SSC	25 (58.1)	10 (23.3)	8 (18.6)	43 (32.1)
SSC	32 (60.4)	11 (20.8)	10 (18.9)	53 (39.6)
Intermediate	4 (25.0)	8 (50.0)	4 (25.0)	16 (11.9)
Degree	0	10 (45.5)	12 (54.5)	22 (16.4)
Total	61 (45.5)	39 (29.1)	34 (25.4)	134 (100.0)

Trainee Involvement and the Type of Job

The following table shows the data relating to involvement of trainee and their job.

Table 5.48
Distribution of Respondents Perceptions on Involvement and Type of Job

Education	*Poor*	*Good*	*Outstanding*	*Total*
Technical	56 (54.4)	25 (24.3)	22 (21.4)	103 (76.9)
Non-technical	5 (16.1)	14 (45.2)	12 (38.7)	31 (23.1)
Total	61 (45.5)	39 (29.1)	34 (25.4)	134 (100.0)

χ^2 = 14.05398 d.f. = 2; p<0.05

An analysis of the data revealed that out of 76.9 per cent of the blue collar respondents, majority (54.4%) rated their involvement as poor, while 45 per cent of them rated it as good to outstanding. Out of the white collar respondents 84.0 per cent of them rated their involvement as good to outstanding. The data suggest that white collar workers' involvement in the programme is more than the blue collar workers.

Trainee Involvement and Experience

The data relating to the involvement of the respondents and their experience levels are presented in the following table.

Table 5.49
Experience and Trainee Involvement

Experience	*Poor*	*Good*	*Very Good*	*Total*
0 to 8 years	22	7	9	38
	(57.9)	(18.4)	(23.7)	(28.4)
9 to 16 years	30	21	12	63
	(47.6)	(33.3)	(19.0)	(47.0)
17 & above	9	11	13	33
	(27.3)	(33.3)	(39.4)	(24.6)
Total	61	39	34	134
	(45.5)	(29.1)	(25.4)	(100.0)

Analysis of the data relating to work experience and trainees' involvement revealed that there is an association between these two variables. Out of respondents having less than eight years of experience, a majority (57.9%) had low levels of involvement. In case of respondents having 9 to 16 years of experience majority of the respondents (47.0%) had rated their involvement as poor. Out of the respondents having 17 years and above work experience a large number (39.40%) had rated their involvement as very good. From this table it is observed that there is low levels of involvement among younger respondents and high level of involvement among senior workers.

Communication

The respondents' perceptions of the communication used in the training programme are presented in the following table.

Table 5.50
Distribution of Respondents' Opinion Regarding Communication Used in the Training Programme

Perceptions	*Frequency*	*Percentage*
Poor	37	27.6
Good	45	33.6
Outstanding	52	38.8
Total	134	100.0

Regarding the communication used in the training programme a large number of the respondents (38.8%) perceived the type of communication used in the programme as outstanding. About 34 per cent of them felt that the communication is good. The remaining said it is poor.

Communication and Age

In the following table the data relating to the perceptions of the respondents towards communication used in the programme and their ages are presented.

Table 5.51
Respondents Perception Towards Communication and Age

Age	*Poor*	*Good*	*Outstanding*	*Total*
20 to 30 years	6 (18.2)	12 (36.4)	15 (45.5)	33 (24.6)
31 to 40 years	23 (31.5)	22 (30.1)	28 (38.4)	73 (54.5)
41 & above	8 (28.6)	11 (39.3)	9 (32.1)	28 (20.9)
Total	37 (27.6)	45 (33.6)	52 (38.8)	134 (100.0)

$\chi^2 = 2.71$; d.f. = 4; $p<0.05$

The results of the analysis of data revealed that there is no association between the two variables, *i.e.*, age and communication. There is no variation in the opinions of the respondents of different age groups.

Communication and Level of Education

The data relating to the educational qualification and the communication are presented in the following table.

Table 5.52
Respondents Perception Towards Communication and Education

Education	*Poor*	*Good*	*Outstanding*	*Total*
Below SSC	8	18	17	43
	(18.6)	(41.9)	(39.5)	(32.1)
SSC	11	16	26	53
	(20.8)	(30.2)	(49.1)	(39.6)
Intermediate	4	6	6	16
	(25.0)	(37.5)	(37.5)	(11.6)
Degree	14	5	3	22
	(63.6)	(22.7)	(13.6)	(16.4)
Total	37	45	52	134
	(27.6)	(33.6)	(38.8)	(100.0)

$\chi^2 = 19.4892$; d.f. = 6; $p<0.05$

Analysis of the data revealed that of the respondents with below SSC education, a large number (41.9%) perceived the communication used in the programme as good. Nearly 50 per cent of the SSC respondents, and a large number of intermediate respondents also rated it as outstanding. However, in case of respondents having degree qualification a majority (63.6%) rated it as poor.

From this table it is observed that the respondents with below degree qualification had rated the communication outstanding, while respondents having degree qualification rated the communication as poor.

The chi-square test revealed that there is an association

between the respondents' qualification and their perception of towards communication.

Communication and Type of Job

The information relating to the communication and type of job of the respondents is presented in the following table.

Table 5.53
Distribution of Respondents Perception Towards Communication and Type of Job

Type of Job	*Poor*	*Good*	*Outstanding*	*Total*
Technical	21 (20.4)	36 (35.0)	46 (44.7)	103 (76.9)
Non-technical	16 (51.6)	9 (29.0)	6 (19.4)	31 (23.1)
Total	37 (27.6)	45 (33.6)	52 (38.8)	134 (100.0)

χ^2 = 12.5944; d.f. = 2; p<0.05

The data revealed that out of 76.9 per cent of the blue collar respondents, a large number of them (44.7%) rated the communication as outstanding. In case of white collar worker respondents, a majority (51.6%) of them rated communication as poor.

Communication and Work Experience

The data relating to the communication and the respondents experience are presented in the following table.

An analysis of the data revealed that out of the respondents having less than eight years of experience a large number (44.7%) rated as outstanding. In case of respondents having 9 to 16 years of experience about 37 per cent perceived the communication as good, where as respondents with 17 years and above 42 per cent rated the communication as good.

Table 5.54
Distribution of Respondents Perception Towards Communication and Work Experience

Work Experience	*Poor*	*Good*	*Very Good*	*Total*
Below 8 years	10 (26.3)	11 (28.9)	17 (44.7)	38 (28.4)
9 to 16 years	19 (30.2)	23 (36.5)	21 (33.3)	63 (47.0)
17 & above	8 (24.2)	11 (33.3)	14 (42.4)	33 (24.6)
Total	37 (27.6)	45 (33.6)	52 (38.8)	134 (100.0)

χ^2 = 1.653; d.f. = 4; p<0.05

The worker-teacher training programme envisaged the employment of the following teaching methods.

(a) Communication Methods-I	:	Lecture, Two-way communications
(b) Communication Methods-II	:	Symposium, panel discussion, debate.
(c) Group Methods	:	Seminar, Role play, conference
(d) Self-study Methods	:	Case study, workshop, programmed instruction.
(e) Audio-visual Aids	:	Film strips, slides, flip chart, graphics, radio, tape-recorder, films, television.

To know to what extent the above methods have been used, data were collected from the respondents about the methods used in the training programme.

The data revealed that lecture method was prominently used, while participatory teaching methods like seminar and role-play were not at all used. After lecture method, group discussions were reported to have been used considerably

(47.0%) while other participatory methods like symposium, debate, seminar and role-play were not used at all. Among audio-visual aids, only charts and other things were used.

Table 5.55
Teaching Aids used in Worker-Teacher Training

Teaching Method	*Considerably used*	*Somewhat used*	*Not used*	*Total*
Lectures	134 (100)	—	—	134
Symposium	5 (3.7)	10 (7.4)	119 (88.9)	134
Debate	20 (14.9)	34 (25.3)	80 (59.8)	134
Seminar	8 (6.0)	14 (10.4)	112 (83.6)	134
Role Play	10 (7.4)	24 (17.9)	100 (74.7)	134
Group discusssions	63 (47.0)	46 (34.3)	25 (18.7)	134
Audio-visual	15 (11.2)	50 (37.3)	69 (51.5)	134

The type of training, the methods used and the techniques adopted are very relevant issues in the learning process. An adult learner may not prefer to sit and listen to long lectures. He needs focussing to express his ideas. In such a situation, lecture, as an effective method of education, has very little relevance. What is needed is a blend of various techniques in the right proportion taking into consideration what the group wants. Over emphasis on a single method should be avoided as far as possible. In workers' education how ever, major prominence was given to lecture method. Virmani[15] (1986), Mathur[16] (1982) favoured the employment of participatory methods of teaching that will make the classes interesting.

Summary

An overview of the results presented in Section C of the present chapter on training component revealed that a majority of the respondents reported that the present duration is less. More prominently young and old workers, blue-collared and less educated favoured extension of the period. A large number of worker-teachers rated the coverage as poor. Cross tabulated analysis shows that higher educated respondents rated the coverage poor while others rated it as good. With regard to trainee involvement a large number felt the level of inputs as advanced. Young, less educated and technical workers considered the level of inputs advanced. Quantity of material supplied was rated more than sufficient. Higher educated and non-technical considered the quality of material as poor. A large number of them rated their involvement in the programme as poor. Particularly blue-collared and less experienced workers found their involvement below par. With regard to communication it was rated as outstanding by less educated and technical workers.

The data suggest that perceptions of young less educated and blue collared workers are at variance with that of better educated and white collared workers. These variations in their perceptions call for the need to have homogenous group of trainees. The homogeneity of the group in terms of education and the type of job facilitate effective learning and trainers will also find it easy to train a homogeneous group and they can tune their methods of teaching in accordance with the composition of the group.

SECTION - D

Unit Level Classes (ULC)

In the third stage of the workers' education programme the worker-teacher has to conduct the unit level classes at the unit or factory or establishment. The duration of the course at the unit level is usually of three months, at the rate of one hour a day for five days in a week, where facilities are available full time unit classes of three week duration are also conducted. The unit level classes can be run by a single worker-teacher or two or more worker-teachers, jointly or by the management, itself with the help of outside faculty. Management should give "time-off", both to the worker-teacher and to the workers to attend classes.

The data revealed that 54.5 per cent of the respondents conducted classes for one batch of the workers at the unit level, followed by 28.3 per cent who conducted classes for 3-4 batches, 10.4 per cent for 5-6 batches and remaining 6.8

per cent conducted 7 and above batches. The highest number of batches taught is 10 and the average is 2.5 which is significant. In some units the managements organise unit level classes, continually for 3 weeks by providing the necessary faculty while the worker-teachers only helped the management in organising unit level classes. But their involvement in this regard is kept low and the worker-teacher takes credit for organising the ULC. Such batches are also included in the number of ULC's conducted by the worker-teachers. In some cases two or three worker-teachers jointly undertake unit level classes.

Table 5.56
Number of Batches Taken by the Worker-Teacher

No. of Batches	*Frequency*	*Percentage*
1 to 2	73	54.5
3 to 4	38	28.3
5 to 6	14	10.4
7 and above	9	6.8
Total	134	100.0

Mean 2.5; Minimum 1 batch; Maximum 10 batches

The workers after undergoing worker-teacher training in the regional centre are expected to conduct unit level classes for all the workers of the unit. The data on the number of worker-teachers taking classes currently are presented in the following table.

Table 5.57
Distribution of Respondents Who are Conducting Unit Level Classes

Response	*Frequency*	*Percentage*
Yes	21	15.7
No	113	84.3
Total	134	100.0

An analysis of the data revealed that an overwhelming majority of the respondents were not conducting unit level classes at the time of the collection of the data. Only about 16 per cent of the respondents are taking classes.

The reasons for not conducting unit level classes were also probed and the data are presented in the following table.

Table 5.58
Reasons for not Undertaking Unit Level Classes

Reasons	*Frequency*	*Percentage*
No time	14	10.4
No interest	8	6.0
Lack of facilities	3	2.2
Non-cooperation of union	36	26.9
Non-cooperation of management	45	33.6
Meager Honorarium	7	5.2
Not applicable	21	15.7
Total	134	100.0

The prime reason for not conducting unit level classes according to one-third of the respondents is the non-cooperation of the management, whereas nearly 27 per cent attributed to non-cooperation of the union. Other causes include were lack of time, disinterest etc. From this, it is evident that the non-cooperation of the supportive organisations is responsible for the under utilisation of the worker-teachers at the last stage, *i.e.* the actual implementation stage.

Selection of Participants in the ULC

The workers' education programme, does not specify any educational qualifications for attending either the worker-teacher training or unit level class. The selection of participants at the unit level classes is left to the worker-teachers who organise classes for them. If the management does not involve itself in conducting unit level classes, it generally leaves it to the worker-teachers to select workers for unit level classes.

Table 5.59
Criteria Followed by the Worker-Teacher in Selecting the Worker for Unit Level Classes

Interest	*Frequency*	*Percentage*
Evinces interest/voluntarily	66	49.3
Management nomination	20	14.9
Union nomination	12	8.9
Education	13	9.7
Experience	23	17.2
Total	134	100.0

An analysis of the data revealed that around 50.0 per cent of the worker-teachers reported that they select those workers who evince interest in the programme who come forward voluntarily. About 15 per cent of the worker-teachers reported that the selection of the workers for the unit level classes is made by the management and nearly nine per cent of the worker-teachers told that, in exceptional cases it is the union which nominates workers for the unit level classes.

Apart from the union/management nomination, 17.2 per cent of the worker-teachers select the workers based on experience, while 9.7 per cent of the worker-teachers select workers who have minimum educational qualifications.

In the industrial units where there are training institutes the managements enable the training institute to conduct unit level classes. In the present study it was found that 14.9 per cent of the worker-teachers have no role in selecting the workers for the unit level classes. Instead, the management selected them and organised unit level classes by involving the worker-teachers.

It is found that the management of a public sector organisation organises unit level classes in the months of February and March, when the industrial activity is in full swing and financial year closes by March 31. The workers whose presence in the factory hampers production, are sent for ULC and later on study tour to keep them away from the work place. The unit level classes come handy for the management.

In another case it was reported that the worker-teachers resort to some unconventional methods to attract workers to the unit level classes. The worker-teacher sends a circular to the workers informing that he is taking them to Mumbai or some other industrial centre and asks them to give their names. He organises a batch of workers for the unit level classes, conducts classes for one day and arranges the visit of the Education Officer on the same day. The classes will not be continued thereafter and after 3 months he takes them on a study tour, taking advantage of the financial benefits and casual leave provided by the management.

Reasons

Table 5.60
Reasons for Workers Undergoing Training in ULC as Perceived by the Worker-Teachers

Reasons	*Frequency*	*Percentage*
To gain knowledge	54	40.3
Study tour	51	38.0
Union pressure	10	7.5
Management nomination	19	14.2
Total	134	100.0

The worker-teachers were asked to give reasons for workers joining the workers' education programme. The answers to this question are presented in the above table.

Out of the 134 sample worker-teachers, a large percentage (40.3%) have said that workers join the scheme to gain knowledge, while 38.0 per cent frankly admitted that study tour/industrial tour which will be conducted after the completion of training programme is the main attraction for the workers to join the scheme. The remaining 21.7 per cent of the respondents were of the view that the workers joined the scheme because they were nominated either by the management or the union.

Attendance

The attendance at the unit level classes was also probed and the responses of the worker-teachers to this item are presented in the following table.

Table 5.61
Attendance at Unit Level Classes

Attendance	*Frequency*	*Percentage*
0 to 20	14	10.4
20 to 40	28	20.9
40 to 60	45	33.6
60 to 80	35	26.1
80 to 100	12	9.0
Total	134	100.0

Mean : 51

The analysis of the data in the table revealed that 35.1 per cent of the worker-teachers reported that their unit level classes were attended by 60 to 100 per cent of the workers. While 33.3 per cent used to have less than 40.0 per cent attendance and the remaining 33.6 per cent reported an attendance ranging from 40 to 60 per cent.

Table 5.62
Regularity of Unit Level Classes

Regularity	*Frequency*	*Percentage*
Regularly Conducted	70	52.2
Irregularly Conducted	50	37.3
Do not know	14	10.5
Total	134	100.0

Majority of the worker-teachers (52.2%) informed that the unit level classes were conducted regularly.

The researcher made visits to the unit level classes along with the education officer and sometimes without education officer. There was full attendance at the unit level classes during visit made along with education officer while the second visit by the researcher without Education Officer found thin attendance at the unit level classes.

For conducting unit level classes, the CBWE gives Rs. 100/- to the worker-teachers as honorarium. The views of the respondents on this item are presented in the following table.

Table 5.63

Opinion on Honorarium

Response	*Frequency*	*Percentage*
Satisfied	44	32.8
Not satisfied	90	67.2
Total	134	100.0

The data in the table revealed that majority of (67.2%) the respondents were not satisfied with the honorarium which stands at Rs. 100/- per month while 32.8 per cent of them were satisfied with the honorarium. The worker-teachers were also asked to specify the amount of honorarium that should be given and their views on this item are presented below.

Table 5.64

Minimum Honorarium

Minimum Honorarium (In Rs. per month)	*Frequency*	*Percentage*
150 to 200	28	31.0
201 to 250	52	57.8
251 to 300	10	11.2
Total	90	100.0

N = 90

The data in the table revealed that all the 90 worker-teachers who were not satisfied with the present honorarium wanted the honorarium to be increased to Rs. 150 - Rs. 300. Out of the 90 respondents who specified the minimum honorarium to be offered to the worker-teachers, 31.0 per cent of the worker-teachers wanted the honorarium to be between Rs. 150 to Rs. 200, while 69.0 per cent of them wanted the same between Rs. 201 to Rs. 300. The average honorarium demanded by the worker-teachers came to Rs. 201. Some worker-teachers demanded payment of conveyance allowance. Some suggested a matching grant equivalent to that of honorarium be given by the management to the worker-teachers. One worker-teacher suggested incentives or increments be given to the worker-teacher who undertake unit level classes.

Syllabus

There is no separate syllabus for unit level classes. The syllabus of the worker-teachers training programme has to be followed in the unit level classes. Flexibility is allowed, and the needs of local industries can also be taken into consideration while framing the syllabus for unit level classes. The worker-teachers' views on the syllabus for the ULC have been elicited and are presented below.

Table 5.65
Perception on the Syllabus of ULC

Perceptions	*Frequency*	*Percentage*
Less	70	52.2
Just right	42	31.4
More	22	16.4
Total	134	100.0

The data in the table revealed that a majority (52.2%) of the worker-teachers were of the opinion that the content of the present syllabus for the ULC is less. While 31.4 per cent of them said that the syllabus is just right and the remaining 16.4 per cent opined that syllabus is too lengthy and needs to be shortened.

Duration of the ULC

The views of the workers on the duration of the ULC were elicited and are presented in the following table.

Table 5.66
Opinion on the Present Duration of Training in ULC

Opinion	*Frequency*	*Percentage*
Wanted duration to be extended	88	65.7
Present duration is sufficient	46	34.3
Total	134	100.0

It can be seen from the table that majority (65.7%) of the worker-teachers wanted the present duration of the training to be increased as it is too short a period to cover the syllabus, while the remaining 34 per cent of the workers felt that it is sufficient. Further inquiries with the worker-teachers revealed that almost all the worker-teachers favoured full time classes, instead of part-time classes of one hour duration for a period of three months, as they give scope for flexibility and continuity in arranging the classes and to enforce attendance.

Cooperation Extended by the Management, Union and Education Officers

Workers perception of the support and encouragement they receive from their management and trade union leadership is a very important aspect. A worker gets motivated to learn further if he feels that he is fully supported by management and union.

The success of Workers' Education Scheme depends very much on the cooperation of the supportive organisations *viz.* management, trade unions, board and participants in the ULC. The worker-teacher needs the support of all the above for smooth conduct of unit level classes. Worker-teachers' perception of the cooperation extended by these organisations was elicited and is presented in the following table.

Table 5.67
Satisfaction with the Management

Level of Satisfaction	*Frequency*	*Percentage*
Satisfied	62	46.3
Can not say	9	6.7
Dissatisfied	63	47.0
Total	134	100.0

The data in the table revealed that a large number (47.0%) of the respondents were dissatisfied with the cooperation extended by the management. While the same percentage of the respondents (46.3%) were satisfied with the cooperation of the management and the remaining 6.7 per cent did not express any opinion in this regard.

There are certain basic facilities without which organisation of training programme is not possible. The management should give time-off to both the worker-teacher and the workers, and the necessary infrastructure for conducting unit level classes. Apart from the physical facilities, the management can support the programme in the shape of supervision of attendance, arrangement of guest lectures, and rewarding trainees for their outstanding performance.

In practice not many managements show any such interest. One reason why worker teachers are unable to conduct unit level classes is lack of support from the management. Another factor, which prevents the management from extending full cooperation to the programme, is their fear that the workers may turn rebellious after undergoing the training programme.

But in most cases, the management and trade unions have different perceptions towards the programme of workers education. The workers who are sent for training are well aware of the cold reception of their management and trade union leaders and hence do not take particular interest in the training. Very few managements and trade unions give serious thought to the workers' education scheme. So more so they just select candidates at random and without any selection criteria and send them for training. What is more, once they are sent, nobody bothers to ensure whether the workers attend the classes or make any effort to learn from the training (Virmani, 1986)[17].

Satisfaction with Trade Unions

Trade unions play an important role in conducting unit level classes. As workers' education programme is essentially aimed at enhancing the general awareness of the workers, the trade union leadership is expected to offer full support to the worker-teacher to conduct unit level classes. The union can have meetings with the worker-teachers, the leaders offer lectures and constant meetings with the worker-teachers. These exercises instill confidence among them and motivate the worker-teachers to perform better. The extent of cooperation offered by the trade union was elicited from the worker-teachers and is presented in the following table.

Table 5.68
Worker-Teachers Satisfaction Level with the Trade Union

Level of Satisfaction	*Frequency*	*Percentage*
Satisfied	73	54.5
Can not say	14	10.4
Dissatisfied	47	35.1
Total	134	100.0

The data revealed that a majority (54.5%) of the worker teachers expressed satisfaction with the help rendered by the unions in conducting unit level classes. 35 per cent of the worker-teachers expressed dissatisfaction and the remaining (10.4%) maintained a neutral stand. It is surprising to note that the worker-teachers, who were nominated/ sponsored by their unions, were dissatisfied with the union's role or support. Workers' education programmes are meant to create awareness among workers and the union is expected to provide whole-hearted support to the programme that enlightens its workers.

Table 5.69
Unions Affiliation of the Worker-Teacher and Satisfaction with the Support Offered to the Programme by Union

Type of the Union	*Satisfied*	*Cant say*	*Dissatisfied*	*Total*
Left	7 (21.9)	1 (3.1)	24 (75.0)	32 (23.9)
Centre	48 (64.9)	9 (12.2)	17 (23.0)	74 (55.2)
Right	18 (64.3)	4 (14.3)	6 (21.4)	28 (20.9)
Total	73 (54.5)	14 (10.4)	47 (35.1)	134 (100.0)

χ^2 = 29.56; d.f. 4; p = <.05

Cross tabulated analysis of the data on the levels of satisfaction regarding the support given by union and the type of the union revealed that three fourths (75.0%) of the worker-teachers belonging to the leftist union expressed dissatisfaction with the unions with regard to its workers' education programmes. In case of centrist unions (INTUC and HMS Unions), nearly two thirds (64.9%) of the worker-teachers expressed satisfaction with the union, and a similar trend is observed among worker-teachers belonging to the rightist unions. The finding that the leftist union leadership is opposed to the workers' education programme is significant, considering the fact that leftist unions are generally perceived as real working class organisations to whom safeguarding the interests of the working class is dear to their heart. The militant leftist unions tend to perceive workers' education programme as a ploy by the management to distract the attention of the workers from fighting for their rights.

In the light of the above finding, it may not be out of context to narrate the experience of the researcher with the leader of a leftist union. When the researcher met the General Secretary of a leftist union in connection with the research work to elicit his views on workers' education, he flared up and said that "the workers' education programme is a bogus programme. The workers without any educational background, after undergoing worker-teacher-training programme, are questioning the leadership and launching separate unions". The leftist union leaders, apprehending threat to their leadership from the trained workers, are creating hurdles or discouraging their worker-teachers to conduct union level classes. It seems that the trade union leaders who develop vested interest in the organisation nurture secret misgiving in genuine development of leadership qualities among workers. The iron law of oligarchy propounded by Robert Michels[18] (1959), in his treatise on political parties is very much operative. Unions though avowed to function democratically, the union leaders distort unions into oligarchies. The union leaders who become power brokers seek to perpetuate themselves in their positions for their own aggrandizement and impose their own will in all union matters.

Satisfaction with Education Officers

The Education Officers act as field officers/organisers in promoting unit level classes, besides acting as instructors at the regional centres. The education officers are entrusted with the responsibility of organising unit level classes in the units that are allocated to them. The targets for different types of programmes are fixed by CBWE, Nagpur and it is stipulated that the education officer must achieve the targets. To meet the targets he persuades the management to allow the worker-teachers to conduct unit level classes in their units. The Education Officers have to maintain good rapport with the worker-teachers who can help them in achieving their targets, by organising unit level classes. He/she is expected to supervise the unit level classes.

Table 5.69(A)
Satisfaction with Education Officer

Satisfaction Level	*Frequency*	*Percentage*
Satisfied	62	46.3
Can not say	9	6.7
Dissatisfied	63	47.0
Total	134	100.0

Data in the table shows that a large number (47.0%) of the respondents were dissatisfied with the Education Officer's role in conducting unit level classes, while equal number of workers (46.3%) were satisfied with them. The finding that 46 per cent of the worker-teachers were satisfied with the Education Officer may be due to the good rapport the Education Officer establishes with the worker-teachers. The worker-teachers in their interviews with the researcher charged the Education Officers with poor supervision of the ULC and corrupt practices. It is alleged that the education officer visits the industry once in a year to take a class in the ULC. Though the education officer is expected to make a surprise visit but her/his visit will be intimated in advance and the worker-teachers manage to have full attendance on that particular day. Some of them were critical of casual attitude of the education officers towards attendance, examinations etc. Similar observations and critical comments were also made in Virmani's study (1986)[19].

There were allegations, that in order to meet the targets, many a time the figures are inflated on paper without the classes being conducted. Some managements and workers alleged that worker-teachers with the knowledge of Education Officers received money, but in reality, no classes were conducted. These allegations may or may not be true, but the fact remains that too much emphasis on quantitative targets has created some problems.

Summary

An overview of the analysis of the data presented in this section suggest that on an average worker-teacher took 2.5 classes, and the highest number of batches trained is 10. An overwhelming majority of them were not undertaking unit level classes at the time of collection of data and the reasons for not conducting classes are non-cooperation of union and management. With regard to the criteria followed in selecting the workers for the unit level classes, a large number of them reported that they selected the workers who evinced interest in the programme and they reported that for gaining knowledge only workers join the programme. The attendance at the unit level classes show that classes have an average of 51 per cent attendance. Majority of the worker teacher reported that unit level classes were conducted regularly. With regard to the honorarium, more than two-thirds of them were not happy with it and they wanted the honorarium to be around Rs. 200/-. The respondents were of the view that the syllabus is less and it needs to be enhanced and the duration of unit level classes be extended. With regard to the cooperation extended by the management, union and education officer the responses were mixed.

SECTION - E

Worker-Teacher Perceptions Towards Other Aspects of the Programme

In this section the perceptions of the worker teachers on different aspects of the programme are presented. These responses were cross-checked by the views of the management, union and worker-trainees in the next chapter.

Some statements have been developed based on the finding of the earlier studies and in-depth interviews with a cross section of the functionaries associated with the programme. The answers to the statements were structured and the answers are as follows: (1) Agree (2) Disagree (3) No comment. These answers are not given any score.

Table 5.70

Responses to the Statement Managements are not Interested in Workers Education

Responses	*Frequency*	*Percentage*
Agree	63	47.0
Disagree	28	20.9
No comment	43	32.1
Total	134	100.0

The responses to the statement that 'managements are not interested in workers education' show that large number of respondents (47%) agreed with the statement while 21 per cent did not agree with this statement. The remaining (32.1%) have not offered any opinion. The above statement was cross-tabulated with the ages of respondents to know whether there is any difference in the responses corresponding to the variable age.

Table 5.71

Age and Responses to the Statement that the Managements are not Interested in Workers' Education Programme

Age	*Responses to the statement*			
	Agree	*Disagree*	*No comment*	*Total*
20 - 30	10	6	17	33
	(30.3)	(18.2)	(51.5)	(24.6)
31 - 40	36	15	22	73
	(49.3)	(20.5)	(30.1)	(54.5)
41+	17	7	4	28
	(60.7)	(25.0)	(14.3)	(20.9)
Total	63	28	43	134
	(47.0)	(20.9)	(32.1)	(100.0)

χ^2 = 12.39; d.f. 4; p = <.05

The data in the table show that out of 24.6 per cent of the respondents whose age is below 30 years, majority of them (51.5%) did not offer any comment on the statement. In the 31 to 40 years age cohort around 50 per cent did agree with the statement, while 20.5 per cent disagreed with the statement. In the higher age cohort of 41+ a large number of the respondents (60.7%) agreed with the statement, with only 14.3 per cent did not offer any opinions and a substantial number of respondents around (25.0%) did not agree with the statement.

The data in the table suggest that as the age increases the percentage of respondents agreeing with the statement that "the management is not interested in workers' education" is increasing. This may be due to the fact that the aged employees are better aware of the tactics played by the employers than the young workers.

Educational status of the respondents and the responses to the statement were cross tabulated and are presented below.

Table 5.72

Education and Responses to the Statement that the Management is not Interested in Workers' Education Progarmme

Education	*Response*			
	Agree	*Disagree*	*No comment*	*Total*
Below SSC	27 (62.8)	6 (14.0)	10 (23.3)	43 (32.1)
SSC	25 (47.2)	8 (15.1)	20 (37.7)	53 (39.6)
Intermediate	4 (25.0)	6 (37.5)	6 (37.5)	16 (11.9)
Degree	7 (31.8)	8 (36.4)	7 (31.8)	22 (16.4)
Total	63 (47.0)	28 (20.9)	43 (32.1)	134 (100.0)

χ^2 = 13.20; d.f. p = <.05

The data in the table revealed that out of the respondents whose educational qualifications are below X standard (Secondary School Certificate) majority of them (62.8%) agreed with the statement while around 14.0 per cent disagreed and the rest did not choose to comment. In case of SSC category respondents a large number (47.2%) of them agreed with the statement. In the intermediate category a large number (37.5%) of them did not agree. In case of degree and above qualified respondents a large number (36.7%) of them did not agree with this statement.

The data suggest that lesser educated workers are perceiving the management negatively, while workers with higher educational qualifications are very cautious in their judgements. On the management interest in workers' education in both categories *i.e.* responents with intermediate and degree qualifications, the percentage of non-committal responses ranged from 23.3 to 37.7 per cent. Lesser-educated respondents negatively perceived the management's interest in workers' education while higher educated are less likely to perceive it negatively. The reason for the negative perception among the lesser educated is that in their enthusiasm to impart education to their brethren, the managements efforts may be falling short of their expectations.

Unions are not Interested in Workers' Education Programme

It was mentioned earlier that the smooth conduction of unit level classes depends on the extent of cooperation extended by the management, union, education officer and the trainee. Trade union is one of the important agencies that facilitates or hinders any programme. To know how the worker-teachers perceive the union perception towards workers' education, a statement that 'union is not interested in workers' education programme' has been presented to them and the answers to this statement are presented in the following table.

Table 5.73

Responses to the Statement Unions are not Interested in Workers' Education Programme

Responses	*Frequency*	*Percentage*
Agree	68	50.7
Disagree	44	32.8
No comment	22	16.5
Total	134	100.0

It is pertinent to note that the workers teachers perceived the unions negatively as they know the true colours of the unions because of their constant association with the unions for undertaking unit level classes. The views of the respondents on the statement were cross-tabulated with the type of job and the same are presented below.

Table 5.74

Job-Wise Distribution of the Responses to the Statement that Union is Not Interested in Workers' Education Programme

Education	*Response*			
	Agree	*Disagree*	*No comment*	*Total*
Technical	45 (43.7)	40 (38.8)	18 (17.5)	106 (76.9)
Non-technical	23 (74.2)	4 (12.9)	4 (12.9)	31 (23.1)
Total	68 (50.7)	44 (32.8)	22 (16.5)	134 (100.0)

χ^2 = 9.55; d.f. = 3; p = <.05

The data in the table suggest that non-technical job holders hold negative views about the unions' interest in workers' education programme as three-fourths (74.2%) of the non-technical job holders agreed with the statement that unions are not interested in workers' education programme. In case of technical job holders a large number (43.7%) agreed with it.

No Follow-up Programmes are Drawn by the Management

The responses of the worker-teachers on the above statement are presented in the following table.

Table 5.75

Responses to the Statements no Follow up Programmes are Drawn by the Management

Responses	*Frequency*	*Percentage*
Agree	77	57.5
Disagree	37	27.6
No comment	20	14.9
Total	134	100.0

The data in the table show that majority of the respondents (57.5%) agreed with the statement. From this it is clear that the managements are sponsoring the workers

Table 5.76

Responses to the Statement that No Follow-up Programmes are Drawn by the Management

Job	*Responses*			
	Agree	*Disagree*	*No comment*	*Total*
Technical	60 (58.3)	24 (23.3)	19 (18.4)	103 (76.9)
Non-technical	17 (54.8)	13 (41.9)	1 (3.2)	31 (23.1)
Total	77 (57.5)	37 (27.6)	20 (14.9)	134 (100.0)

χ^2 = 6.74; d.f. 3; p = <.05

for the worker-teacher classes because of the pressure created on them by the Board Officials. The responses to the statement that no follow-up programmes are drawn/ organised by the management are cross-tabulated with the nature of the job of the worker-teacher and presented in the following table.

The data in the table indicate that majority of the respondents in each category agreed with the statement. In case of technical job holders a majority (58.3 %) of them agreed while around 23 per cent disagreed and the remaining (18.4%) did not express any opinion. In the non-technical category of the respondents majority (54.8%) agreed while a substantial number (41.9%) of worker teachers in this category disagreed with the statement. Non-technical job holders perceived negatively the follow-up efforts of the management. As there is no significant difference with regard to their age, experience and union, the cross tables are not presented.

There Should be Some Educational Criteria for Selection of Worker-Teacher

The following table presents the responses of the worker-teachers towards the above statement.

Table 5.77
Responses to the Statement that there Should be Some Education Criteria for the Selection of Worker-Teachers

Responses	*Frequency*	*Percentage*
Agree	53	39.6
Disagree	30	22.4
No comment	51	38.0
Total	134	100.0

The responses to the statement show that a large number (39.6%) of worker-teachers agreed with the statement while 22.4 per cent of the respondents disagreed with the statement and the remaining (38%) did not offer any comment.

The responses to the statement were matched with the educational qualifications to know whether there is any variation in the responses with the differences in educational qualifications.

Table 5.78

Education and Responses to the Statement that Some Education Criteria are to be Followed in Worker-Teacher Selection

Education	*Responses*			
	Agree	*Disagree*	*No comment*	*Total*
Below SSC	11 (25.6)	16 (37.2)	16 (37.2)	43 (32.1)
SSC	22 (41.5)	9 (17.0)	22 (41.5)	53 (39.6)
Intermediate	8 (50.0)	—	8 (50.0)	16 (11.9)
Degree +	12 (54.5)	5 (22.8)	5 (22.7)	22 (16.4)
Total	53 (39.6)	30 (22.4)	51 (38.1)	134 (100.0)

The analysis of the data in the table revealed that a large number of worker-teachers (37.2%) disagreed with the statement while the same percentage of them did not offer any opinion. In case of respondents whose educational qualifications are SSC, a large number of them agreed with the statement that there should be some criteria in the selection of worker-teacher for the training programme. In case of intermediate and degree holders a majority of them agreed with the statement. It may be deduced from the data that highly educated respondents, are more critical of the present procedure of selecting the workers for the training programme.

There are some trade union leaders who feel that since the syllabus is management oriented and it is against the unions and its leadership they are not interested in training of workers or in the workers' education programme. The sample respondents underwent worker-teacher training and imparted training to the worker at the unit level classes, it was thought they are in a better position to assess the syllabus. They were questioned on the relevance and the nature of syllabus.

Table 5.79
Responses to the Statement "Syllabus is Anti-Management"

Responses	*Frequency*	*Percentage*
Agree	10	7.5
Disagree	114	85.0
No comment	10	7.5
Total	134	100.0

The data in the table showed that an overwhelming majority of the worker-teachers did not agree with the statement that the syllabus is anti-management. Negligible percentage of the worker-teachers (7.5%) agreed with the statement. The impression/belief that the syllabus is anti-management is not supported by the data.

Table 5.80
Responses to the Statement that Syllabus is Anti-Union

Responses	*Frequency*	*Percentage*
Agree	10	7.5
Disagree	113	74.3
No comment	11	8.2
Total	134	100.0

The data in the table clearly show that the syllabus is not anti-union as three-fourths of the worker-teachers disagreed with the statement that the syllabus is anti-union. The data in the above two tables clearly refute the allegation that it is management-biased and anti-union.

As it has been mentioned earlier that the syllabus for workers' education has been modified from time to time in tune with the developments in the organised sector. The syllabus has been modified thrice and the syllabus review committees make efforts to see that the syllabus is relevant. To know the perceptions of the worker-teachers on the relevance of the syllabus, the following statement has been presented to them and the responses are presented in the table.

Table 5.81
Responses to the Statement that Syllabus is not Relevant

Responses	*Frequency*	*Percentage*
Agree	82	61.2
Disagree	42	31.3
No comment	10	7.5
Total	134	100.0

The data in the table show that majority of the respondents agreed with the statement that syllabus is not relevant, around 32 per cent disagreed with it. The worker-teachers having been trained by the board, and trained a number of batches are the right people to comment upon the syllabus. The worker-teachers responses are based on the feedback they get from unit level classes.

Table 5.82
Responses to the Statement "Education Officers are Interested in Targets"

Responses	*Frequency*	*Percentage*
Agree	78	50.7
Disagree	40	29.8
No comment	26	19.5
Total	134	100.0

The data in the table clearly show that education officers were more concerned about achieving their targets as majority of the worker-teacher (50.7%) agreed with the statement. This finding lends credence to the allegation that to meet targets, many a time the figures are inflated on paper, without classes being conducted.

One worker-teacher reported that education officer visits the industry/place where unit level classes are conducted once during the period, takes a class for half an hour and he/she is never seen afterwards. This indicates poor supervision and it needs to be strengthened.

Table 5.83

Responses to the Statement that Workers' Education is Promoting Fighting Culture

Responses	*Frequency*	*Percentage*
Agree	22	16.4
Disagree	87	64.9
No comment	25	18.7
Total	134	100.0

The data on the perceptions of the respondents to the statement that workers' education is promoting fighting culture, suggest majority of the respondents among worker-teachers (64.9%) refute the charge that is leveled against them.

Table 5.84

Responses to the Statement that Worker-Teacher Should Train at Least Two Batches

Responses	*Frequency*	*Percentage*
Agree	100	74.6
Disagree	15	11.2
No comment	19	14.2
Total	134	100.0

A close examination of the responses of the respondents reveals that an overwhelming majority of the worker-teachers (74.6%) supported the statement.

Table 5.85
Responses to this Statement Workers' Education Be Made Compulsory

Responses	*Frequency*	*Percentage*
Agree	99	73.9
Disagree	23	17.1
No comment	12	9.0
Total	134	100.0

Three-fourths of the worker-teachers are in favour of making the scheme compulsory as they found it useful and extend it to all workers in the establishment.

Table 5.86
Responses to the Statement that Trade Unions Should Takeover the Responsibility of Workers Education

Responses	*Frequency*	*Percentage*
Agree	36	26.9
Disagree	87	64.9
No comment	11	8.2
Total	134	100.0

The data in the table show that nearly two-thirds of the worker-teachers did not agree with this statement. This indicates their lack of confidence in the trade unions and its commitment to the cause of education. They may be of the view that the present trade unions are ill equipped or have no capacity or no time to undertake educational programme and they desire that the trade unions should confine themselves to protecting or fighting for the rights and privileges of the workers.

It is surprising to note that the worker-teachers who were active members of the trade unions are opposed to the transfer of workers' education from the board to the unions.

After the completion of the period of training in the unit level classes, the trainees are taken to industrial areas/places situated in the country to make them aware of the industrial development of the country, and to exchange views with fellow workers. This study tour has been perceived as the main attraction for the workers joining the programme. Managements provide advance, special casual leave and other facilities for the workers to undertake the study tour. It has been observed in the circles relating to the workers' education that the discussions in the unit level classes centered around study tour, how to organise it and the places to be visited and the imparting of education is relegated to the second position. There is also widespread opinion among workers that attraction of study tour has kept the programme alive and the moment the facility of industrial tour is withdrawn the programme either collapses or become difficult to be sustained.

To know the views of the respondents on the study tour, the following statement has been presented and the responses to it are presented in the following table.

Table 5.87

Responses to the Statement that the Study Tour is Main Attraction and Without it the Level of Interest in Workers' Education Cannot be Sustained

Responses	*Frequency*	*Percentage*
Yes	54	40.3
No	30	22.4
No comment	50	37.3
Total	134	100.0

The data show that the worker-teachers felt that without study tour the continuation of the programme is difficult.

The worker teacher for conducting unit level classes has

to seek the cooperation of the management, union, education officer and the worker-trainee and in majority of the cases classes are conducted after the end of working hours. His role as worker-teacher some times comes into conflict with his work and to know whether conduction of unit level class has come into conflict with his work and they were asked a question on this aspect. The data are presented in the following table.

Table 5.88
Responses to the Question Whether his Role as Worker-Teacher Comes Into Conflict with his Work

Responses	*Frequency*	*Percentage*
Yes	48	35.8
No	86	64.2
Total	134	100.0

The data show that a significant majority of the respondents informed that conduction of unit level has not come into conflict with his work in the factory while 35.8 per cent of them said conduction of unit level class affects his work.

Whether the worker-teacher's role in conducting unit level comes into conflict with his family responsibilities has been elicited from the respondents and the responses are presented in the following table.

Table 5.89
Responses to the Question Whether his Role as Worker-Teacher Comes Into Conflict with his Family Responsibilities

Responses	*Frequency*	*Percentage*
Yes	49	31.3
No	92	68.7
Total	134	100.0

The data in the table show that more than two-thirds of the respondents did not think that his role of worker-teacher has come into conflict with his family life while 31.3 per cent of them said it has come into conflict with his family.

Summary

A review of the responses of the workers to the other aspects of the programme suggest that a large number (47%) of the respondents did not subscribe to the notion that management is against the workers' education: but majority of the older workers less educated endorsed the view. Majority of the respondents told that unions are against workers education, more particularly the white collared persist with the idea that unions are against workers education. A large majority (57.5%) felt that management does not take up any follow up measures after nominating the workers for worker-teacher training and a large number (40%) felt that there should be prescribed some minimum educational qualifications for undergoing worker-teacher training and around three-fourths of the respondents favoured the idea that the worker-teacher should train at least two batches. With regard to the syllabus majority of the worker-teachers disagreed with the view that it is either anti-management or anti-union. However, they believed that the syllabus is not relevant to the day-to-day requirements of the workers. They felt that workers' education is not promoting fighting culture and favoured the training in workers' education be made compulsory to all workers. They staunchly oppose the transfer of workers' education function to the unions.

References

1. Virmani, B.R. (1986) *Evaluation of Workers' Education* (unpublished report) ASCI, Hyderabad, p. 278.
2. CBWE (1958) *Rules and Regulations of CBWE*, Nagpur.
3. Virmani, B.R. (1986) *Evaluation of Workers' Education* (unpublished report) ASCI, Hyderabad, p. 279.
4. David A. Cecenzo, Stephen P. Robins (1989) *Personnel/Human Resource Management*, Prentice Hall of India, New Delhi. p. 312.

5. Carter V. Good (Ed.) (1959) *Dictionary of Education*, McGraw Hill Company, New York.
6. Govt. of India (1982) *Report of the Syllabus Review Committee on Training Programmes of Central Board for Workers Education*, Ministry of Labour, p. 22.
7. Virmani, B.R. (1986) *Evaluation of Workers' Education* (unpublished report) ASCI, Hyderabad, p. 94.
8. Holmstrom, Mask (1985) *Industry and Inequality: The Social Anthropology of Indian Labour*, Orient Longman, New Delhi.
9. ILO (1985) *An Introductory Course on Teaching and Training Methods for Management Development*, Sterling Publishers (ILO Office), New Delhi, p. 35.
10. ILO (1985) *An Introductory Course on Teaching and Training Methods for Management Development*, Sterling Publishers (ILO Office), New Delhi, p. 36.
11. ILO (1985) *An Introductory Course on Teaching and Training Methods for Management Development*, Sterling Publishers (ILO Office), New Delhi, p. 29.
12. Kubr, M. (1985) *An Introductory Course on Teaching and Training Methods for Management Development*, Sterling Publishers (ILO Office), New Delhi, p. 1.
13. ILO (1985) *An Introductory Course on Teaching and Training Methods for Management Development*, Sterling Publishers (ILO Office), New Delhi, p. 35.
14. Kubr, M. (1985) *An Introductory Course on Teaching and Training Methods for Management Development*, Sterling Publishers (ILO Office), New Delhi, p. 5.
15. Virmani, B.R. (1986) *Evaluation of Workers' Education* (unpublished report) ASCI, Hyderabad, p. 127.
16. Mathur, V.S. (1982) *Workers' Education Today*, ICFTU, Asian Regional Organisation, New Delhi, pp. 15-16.
17. Virmani, B.R. (1986) *Evaluation of Workers'Education* (unpublished report) ASCI, Hyderabad, p. 126.
18. Mitchels, Robert (1959) *Political Parties Translated by Eden & Cedar Paul*, Dover Publications Inc., New York.
19. Virmani, B.R. (1986) *Evaluation of Workers' Education* (unpublished report) ASCI, Hyderabad, p. 95.

6

The Scheme of Workers' Education: Perceptions of Worker-Trainees, Union Officials and Management Personnel

Introduction

The perceptions of the worker-trainees, trade union officials and management personnel were elicited with the purpose of comparing them with the perceptions of the worker-teachers presented in the preceding sections. As stated in the methodology chapter 254 worker-trainees, 106 trade unions officials and 120 management personnel were administered an interview schedule. The analysis of the data collected through the schedule is presented in this section.

Some statements have been developed based on the findings of the earlier studies and in-depth interview with a cross-section of the functionaries associated with the programme. The answers to the statements were structured on a three-point scale and the answers are as follows: (1) Agree (2) Disagree (3) No comment. These answers are not given any score.

Reasons for Workers Joining the Scheme

Workers who undergo training in unit level classes have different motives. Some of them join the scheme to gain knowledge, some attend the classes because they have been sent by the management or persuaded by the union, some enroll in the programme to avail the incentives offered by it. The impact of the programme on the trainees is dependent on the purpose for which the individual workers join the training programme.

Table 6.1
Reasons for Workers Joining the Programme

Reasoning	*Worker Trainees*	*Union Officials*	*Management Personnel*
To gain knowledge	147 (57.9)	58 (54.7)	23 (19.2)
Sent by the management	35 (13.8)	6 (5.7)	18 (15.0)
Sent by the union	12 (4.7)	14 (13.2)	3 (2.5)
Selected by the worker-teacher	18 (7.1)	4 (3.8)	12 (10.0)
Study tour	42 (16.5)	24 (22.0)	64 (53.3)
Total	254	106	120

The data in the table revealed that majority of the worker-trainees (57.9%) and union officials (54.7%) hold the view that the sole purpose of workers attending the unit level classes is their keenness to gain knowledge. Contrary to this view, the management personnel perceive that the study tour is the main attraction. The management perceptions are in tune with the stereotype management has on labour and the union perception is in consonance with the positive views held by the union about labour. Putting aside the two divergent, views it has been pertinent to note that the study tour was perceived as the main reason by only 16.5 per cent of the worker-trainees. This shows that gaining knowledge is the main motive for attending the unit level classes irrespective of the fact whether the management or trade union selected the worker-trainee. Sarma[1] (1980) Unnithan[2] (1990) finding that gaining knowledge is the main factor that motivates the worker to join in the Workers' education programme has corroborated this, while Virmani[3] (1986) suggest that study tour is the main attraction.

Duration of Unit Level Classes

The unit level classes in the industrial establishments, where the programme of Workers' education is implemented, are conducted in two ways.

(a) One-hour class at the end of the working hours for a period of three months.

(b) Three weeks full time classes.

In majority of the industries, the unit level classes are held after working hours for a period of three months. During this period the worker-teacher is expected to cover the syllabus which is similar to that of the worker-teacher training. It varies in details and emphasis. To know whether the duration of the unit level classes is sufficient or not, the respondents were asked to spell out their views.

Table 6.2
Duration of Unit Level Classes

Reasoning	*Worker Trainee*	*Union Officials*	*Management*
Less	132 (52.0)	14 (13.2)	19 (15.8)
Just right	89 (35.0)	18 (17.0)	15 (12.5)
Much	23 (9.0)	6 (5.7)	48 (40.0)
Do not know	10 (4.0)	68 (64.1)	38 (31.7)
Total	254	106	120

The percentages are in parenthesis

The data in the table on the duration of training revealed that majority of the worker-trainees (52.0%) reported that the duration of the training is less. While trade union officials who are less familiar with the syllabus and other details of the programme pleaded ignorance and the management respondents felt that the duration is to be curtailed as they have to spare workers daily for half an hour before the close of the working hours. The responses of the worker-trainees have been in tune with the responses of the worker-teachers who also feel that the present duration is less and needs to be extended. The enquiries made by the researcher further revealed that majority of the worker-trainees preferred full time classes as it facilitates continuity and acquisition of knowledge at a faster pace. It ensures close supervision and involvement by the management and it goes a long way in improving the quality of the training programme.

Regularity of Unit Level Classes

The unit level classes can be conducted daily for one hour after working hours for 3 months or full time classes continuously. Conduction of unit level classes, in majority of the industries, is left to the worker-teacher and in one or two industries the management takes up the responsibility of conducting unit level classes with the help of the worker-teachers.

Wherever management takes up, it conducts the unit level classes continuously drawing faculty from the management personnel. In case, the management does not conduct the classes, it has to provide accommodation for classes. The one-hour duration class time has to be shared by both management and the worker. The management gives half an hour time-off to the workers to attend the classes and it is also expected to supervise the unit level classes. Regularity of unit level classes facilitates the transfer of knowledge and keeps the interest of the trainee alive. But conducting classes depends on the cooperation extended by the management, union, interest and motivation of the trainee and the personality of the worker-teacher. Here an attempt is made to probe how regularly the unit level classes were held. The perceptions of the respondents are presented below.

The data in the table 6.3 show that a majority (64.2%) of the worker-trainees reported irregularity in conducting the classes. Majority of respondents among trade union officials and management personnel pleaded ignorance about the way the classes were conducted (58.5% and 43.3%). The above finding does not support the fact that majority of the worker-teachers said that unit level classes were conducted regularly.

Table 6.3
Duration of Unit Level Classes

Regularity	*Respondents*		
	Worker-Trainee	*Union*	*Management*
Regularly Conducted	71 (27.9)	34 (32.1)	48 (40.0)
Irregularly Conducted	163 (64.2)	10 (9.4)	20 (16.7)
Do not know	20 (7.9)	62 (58.5)	52 (43.3)
Total	254	106	120

The fact that the majority of the worker-trainees reporting irregularity in conducting unit level classes lends credence to the charges often made against the board that the reported progress made by it is only on paper and in reality the picture is different. It may not be out of context to recall the experience of the researcher in one of the industries in which hundreds of worker-trainees are claimed to have been trained at the unit level classes. The personnel manager of an undertaking expressed surprise on being told by the researcher that unit level classes were held in his organisation and hundreds of workers were trained in the unit level classes. He was not aware of the programmes conducted by the board in his own organisation. The manager on being told by some one that the worker-teacher is organising classes in trade union office the researcher contacted the secretary of the trade union who expressed ignorance about the said programme. In the course of the interview some one in the office reminded him that Mr. David was taking classes. It has also come to the notice of the researcher how the unit level classes are being abused for furtherance of one's greed. In one of the organisations the worker-teacher taking advantage of the perks provided by the management for study tour, sent a circular to the workers that he intended to take 40 members on a study tour or excursion to one of the cities in India. He urged them to subscribe their names. He gathered 40 members, collected money from them for facilitating the tour and asked the workers to come to the unit level class for one day. He also made sure that on that day the education officer also visited the class. He claimed honorarium for the classes not held by him besides collecting a share out of the study tour grant of the group. The education officer is satisfied that the organisation under his jurisdiction conducts unit level classes. But in practice no classes are held.

Selection of Worker-Teacher

The Workers' education programme did not specify any qualifications for undergoing worker-teacher training. The selection of workers for worker-teacher training has been left to the unions and the union in accordance with its interests nominates workers. As the workers after completion of the training, have to impart what has been learnt in the training programme to the workers in the unit level classes, teaching or imparting knowledge requires certain amount of education, communication abilities and aptitude for teaching. Worker-teacher training also involves use of library, teaching aids and preparation of assignments. All these warrant rational selection of workers for the worker-teacher training for the effective transfer of knowledge in the unit level classes. There has been some criticism against the unions that without following any criteria they are nominating the workers for worker-teacher training. To improve the quality of teaching it has been felt necessary that there should be some minimum education criteria for selection of workers. Their responses to the statement that there should be criteria for worker-teacher training are presented in the following table.

Table 6.4
Responses to the Statement there Should be Some Minimum Educational Qualification as Criteria for Selection of Worker-Teachers

Responses	*Worker Trainee*	*Union Officials*	*Management*
Agree	194 (76.4)	46 (43.4)	68 (56.7)
Disagree	26 (10.2)	29 (27.3)	12 (10.0)
No comment	34 (13.4)	31 (29.3)	40 (33.3)
Total	254	106	120

The responses to the statement revealed that more than three-fourths of the worker-trainees favoured some educational qualification for worker-teacher training and similarly the management respondents agreed with the view that there should be some criteria. Worker-teachers views are at variance. All this indicates that all of them except worker-teachers endorsed the view expressed in the statement. It is pertinent to note the observations of ILO[4] "to train workers to become teachers was an innovative idea.... In order to become successful teachers, those who had worked as machine operators, craftsman or in any other profession now had to learn new skills, adapted to modern methods of teaching to be able to carry on the job of teaching fellow workers at plant level".

Discussions with the trainees revealed that there should be some qualifications prescribed for undergoing the training programme to improve the efficacy of the programme. One worker-trainee suggested that unions should sponsor workers who are genuinely interested in the programme. Some worker-trainees suggested that bachelor degree should be made the minimum qualification. Another worker suggested that the teaching ability and communication skills should be given importance while nominating the workers for worker-teacher training.

Optimum Utilisation of Worker-Teachers

The worker-teacher as the nomenclature denotes, after undergoing training is expected to take unit level classes to the workers in their respective units. Earlier research studies have found that in majority of the cases the worker-teacher's job ends with undergoing training and the worker-teachers are less inclined to take classes in the establishment. Admitting the under utilisation of the teachers, 1981-82 annual report[5] observed during the twenty four years of the activities of the board almost saturation point has been reached in many centres. Many worker-teachers remain either underutilized or unutilized. Under-utilization of worker-teacher means wastage of money spent on training of worker-teachers. "Conducting unit level classes will offset the costs of training them. Optimum utilisation of the worker-teacher will go a long way in accomplishing the objectives and strengthening the programme. It is considered reasonable to expect the teacher to take or train at least two batches of the workers at the units. It has been presented to them and the respondents' perceptions to the statement that worker-teacher should train two batches of workers are analysed in the following table.

Table 6.5
Responses to the Statement that Worker-Teacher Should Train Two Batches

Responses	*Worker Trainee*	*Union Officials*	*Management*
Agree	120 (47.2)	39 (36.8)	29 (24.2)
Disagree	83 (32.7)	52 (49.1)	75 (62.5)
No comment	51 (20.1)	15 (14.1)	16 (13.3)
Total	254	106	120

A close examination of the responses of the respondents revealed that nearly half of the worker-trainees supported the view that worker-teacher should atleast train two batches of students. Management personnel and trade union officials do not subscribe to the same view. Management may not like the idea as it involves more unit level classes and loosing more man-hours. The trade unions may have other ways of utilising the worker-teachers in their organisation. The perceptions of the worker-teachers and trainees are at variance with that of management and union.

Management is not Interested in Workers Education

It has been suggested by the earlier studies and there is a popular notion that the management is not interested in Workers' education as it is not a training programme developed and administered by it and they feel forced to release the workers for worker-teacher training and for unit level classes. Hence here an attempt is made to examine how the respondents of the present study view the role of management in the workers education. The responses to the statement 'management is not interested in workers education' are presented in the following table.

Table 6.6
Responses to the Statement Management is not Interested in Workers Education

Responses	*Worker Trainee*	*Union Officials*	*Management*
Agree	145 (57.1)	56 (52.8)	14 (11.7)
Disagree	76 (29.9)	30 (22.3)	72 (60.0)
No comment	33 (13.0)	20 (14.9)	34 (28.3)
Total	254	106	120

The data in the table revealed that the worker-trainees and trade union officials subscribe to the view that the management is not interested in Workers' education. The management respondents disagreed with the statement. The worker-teachers also subscribe to the view that the management is not interested in Workers' education programme. Expressing similar view, Ramaswamy[6] (1986) observed that inspite of the accommodation of their viewpoint, most employers have been indifferent to the scheme, if not hostile.

No Follow-up Programmes are Drawn by the Management

The management releases the workers nominated by the union for worker-teacher training programme and provide infrastructure for conducting unit level classes. The managements generally assume that their role ends with releasing the worker-teacher. But the management can do many things like proper utilisation of the trained worker-teachers, supervision of unit level classes and drawing up some follow up measures. It has been noticed that many organisations are not drawing any follow up measures. To know how the respondents perceive the follow up programmes of the management, the following statement was presented to them and their responses are analysed below.

Table 6.7
Responses to the Statements no Follow-up Programmes are Drawn by the Management

Responses	*Worker Trainee*	*Union Officials*	*Management*
Agree	77 (57.5)	66 (62.3)	23 (19.2)
Disagree	37 (27.6)	31 (29.2)	52 (43.3)
No comment	20 (14.9)	9 (8.5)	43 (37.5)
Total	254	106	120

The data show that majority of the worker-trainees (57.5%) and union officials (62.3%) agreed with the statement while management personnel disagreed with the same. The worker-teachers also share the perception of worker-trainees and union officials. One worker teacher reported that strict action is to be taken against the workers who are not regular to the class. Monitoring of the classes will improve attendance in the unit.

Unions are not Interested in the Workers Education

It was mentioned in the earlier chapter that for the smooth conduction of unit level classes the support of union is imperative. The board has given greater say to the unions in the workers education. It is the union that nominates the workers for worker-teacher training and the management has to simply release the workers. Union is the ultimate beneficiary of the programme, which enlightens the workers with knowledge and promotes leadership qualities among the workers. To know how the respondents perceive its role in the programme, the respondents were asked 'do you agree' with the statement that 'unions are not interested in Workers' education programme' and the responses to this are presented below.

Table 6.8

Responses to the Statement Unions are not Interested in Workers' Education Programme

Responses	*Worker Trainee*	*Union Officials*	*Management*
Agree	95 (37.4)	22 (20.8)	62 (51.7)
Disagree	45 (17.7)	65 (61.3)	10 (8.3)
No comment	114 (44.9)	19 (17.9)	48 (40.0)
Total	254	106	120

The data in the table revealed that majority of the management (51.7%) respondents endorsed the view that unions are not interested in workers education. Majority of the union respondents disagreed with it. The worker-teachers subscribe to the view that unions are against workers education. Pant[7] (1973) and Ramaswamy[8] (1985) also opined that unions are indifferent to the programme.

Workers' Education is Promoting Fighting Culture

Despite many public pronouncements made by the board that Workers' education is to make the working class responsible and committed, some managements feel that the Workers' education is used to propagate militant trade unionism (Ramaswamy[9], 1985). To know how the respondents of the present study perceive it, they were asked to spell out their views.

Table 6.9

Responses to the Statement that Workers' Education is Promoting Fighting Culture

Responses	*Worker Trainee*	*Union Officials*	*Management*
Agree	78 (30.7)	25 (23.5)	57 (47.5)
Disagree	132 (52.0)	51 (48.1)	42 (35.0)
No comment	44 (17.3)	30 (28.3)	21 (17.5)
Total	254	106	120

The data on the perception of the respondents to the statement that Workers' education is promoting fighting culture refute the charges majority of the respondents among worker-trainees (52.0%) and trade union officials disagreed with the statement, while 47.5 per cent of the management respondents feel that workers are becoming militant after training. The perceptions of worker-trainees and trade union officials validate the perception of worker-teachers who disagree with the statement that Workers' education is promoting fighting culture.

Trade Union Should Takeover the Responsibility of Workers Education

It has been stated that the ultimate objective of Workers' education programme is to enable the trade unions to take over ultimately the function of workers education. In USA and European countries the workers education/labour education is the domain of trade unions. The unions were not strong enough to provide educational function in India hence, the government shouldered the responsibility of providing education to the workers.

The programme has completed 43 years since its inception in 1958, it has been felt that the time is ripe to transfer the educational function to the unions. To know how the respondents perceive the idea of transferring the Workers' education to union the following statement was presented to them and responses are presented in the following table.

Table 6.10
Responses to the Statement "Trade Unions Should Takeover the Responsibility of Workers Education"

Responses	*Worker Trainee*	*Union Officials*	*Management*
Agree	83 (32.7)	40 (37.8)	72 (60.0)
Disagree	99 (39.0)	55 (51.9)	17 (14.2)
No comment	72 (28.3)	11 (10.3)	31 (25.8)
Total	254	106	120

The data in the table show that worker-trainees, union officials did not subscribe to the idea of transferring the function of education to the unions while the management respondents endorsed the idea, implying that job related training programmes are their concern and the union should undertake labour education programmes. The perceptions of trainees and union officials supported the perception of the worker-teachers that Workers' education function should not be given to the unions. The fact that nearly 40.0 per cent of the trade union respondents favoured the idea indicates that unions are not totally averse to this proposal. But Ramaswamy[10] (1986) opined that the prospectus of unions taking over the educational function is bleak. In fact, some centrist unions in the region run well-established training institutes to develop second line leadership in the unions.

Education Officers are Target-Oriented

The education officers act as field officers in promoting unit level classes besides acting as instructors at the regional centres. They are entrusted with the task of organising unit level classes for the workers in the region. A number of programmes, besides promoting unit level classes, are to be conducted every month by the education officers. The targets for different types of programmes are set by the regional directorate in accordance with the targets set by the board for the regional centre. The following table shows the targets set by the regional centre for the education officers.

A close examination of the table revealed that education officers in addition to the programmes meant for organised sector have to conduct and supervise programmes for the unorganised and rural sector.

The data in the table clearly show that education officers were perceived to be more concerned about achieving their targets as majority of the management personnel (56.7%) and nearly half of the worker-trainees reported that they are interested in accomplishing the targets. This finds support to the perception of the worker-teachers that education officers are interested in targets. This finding lends credence to the allegation that to meet targets, many a times the figures

Table 6.11
Regional Directorate of Workers Education, (Visakhapatnam) Targets for the Education Officers (For the Year 1997-98)

S.No.	Name of the course	Total Target		Individual Education Officers Target							
				EO 1	EO 2		EO 3		EO 4		EO 5
1.	Worker-Teacher Training course	1	29	1	9.50		6.50		6.50		6.50
2.	Leadership development course	2	22	–	4.00	1	7.00	1	7.00		4.00
3.	Refresher course for worker teacher	1	3.0							1	2.0
4.	Joint Education programme (3 days)	12	18.0	3	4.50	3	4.50	3	4.50	3	4.5
5.	Need based education	15	15.0	4	4.00	4	4.00	4	4.00	3	3.0
6.	Unit level classes	40	4.0	10	1.00	10	1.00	10	1.00	1	10.0
7.	Joint education programme (2 days)	12	12.0	3	3.00	3	3.00	3	3.00	3	3.0
8.	Need based special course (1 week)	10	1.00	2	0.20	2	0.20	0	0.20	4	0.40
9.	Special programmes on quality of life for workers & their spouses										
	a) 5 days	2	4.0	–				1	2.00	1	2.0
	b) 2 days	2	4.0	1	1.00	1	2.00	–	–	–	–

	Unorganised sector									
1.	Camps for workers in unorganised sector (5 days)	6	12	2	4.00	2	4.00	1	2.00	1	2.0
2.	Camps for workers in weaker sections	6	12	1	2.00	1	2.00	2	4.00	2	4.0
	Rural sector										
1.	Rural awareness camps	32	24	8	6.00	8	6.00	8	6.00	8	6.00
2.	Orientation programme for rural educators	1	2	1	1.00		–	–	–	1	1.00
3.	Special seminars for unorganised sector (2 days)	2	2	–	–	1	1.00	1	1.00	–	–
4.	Special seminars for women (2 days)	2	2	–	–	–	–	1	1.00	1	1.00
5.	Seminar for parents of child labour 2 days	2	2	1	1.00	1	1.00	–	–	–	–
6.	Special seminar for SC/ST workers	2	2	1	1.00	–	–	–	–	–	–

are inflated on paper, without classes being conducted. Kakkar[11] (1973) found that the arrangements for supervising the unit level classes were very poor, resulting in bogus reports from worker-teachers. Virmani[12] (1986) remarked that fixation of targets by headquarters of the CBWE for different types of programmes (including unit level classes) adversely affected the quality of the programme. There were allegations that figures were inflated on paper to satisfy the targets set by higher authorities.

Table 6.12
Responses to the Statement "Education Officers are Interested in Targets"

Responses	*Worker Trainee*	*Union Officials*	*Management*
Agree	124 (48.8)	42 (39.5)	68 (56.7)
Disagree	78 (30.7)	57 (53.8)	38 (31.6)
No comment	52 (20.5)	7 (6.7)	14 (11.7)
Total	254	106	120

Syllabus

The Workers' education programme provided detailed syllabus to the education officers, worker-teachers (detailed discussion on syllabus is made in Chapter I) and unit level classes. The syllabus for worker-teacher training and for unit level classes is same except for some variation in emphasis and details. The syllabus is reviewed from time to time. Flexibility is allowed at the unit level classes and the Regional Advisory Committee has the power to modify or add any item to the syllabus to suit to the regional conditions. Despite all this, in some sections there has been a feeling that syllabus is anti-management or anti-union and it is not relevant to the present day needs of the workers. The respondents' perceptions on the syllabus have been probed and are presented in the following tables.

Table 6.13
Responses to the Statement "Syllabus is Anti-Management"

Responses	*Worker Trainee*	*Union Officials*	*Management*
Agree	48 (18.9)	150 (14.2)	25 (20.8)
Disagree	137 (53.9)	72 (67.9)	67 (55.8)
No comment	69 (27.2)	19 (17.9)	28 (23.4)
Total	254	106	120

The data in the table revealed that majority of the respondents refute the charge that the syllabus is anti-management. The worker-teachers also did not subscribe to the view that syllabus is anti-management. The data in the table suggest there are few takers to the idea that the syllabus is anti-management.

Table 6.14
Responses to the Statement Syllabus is Anti-Union

Responses	*Worker Trainee*	*Union Officials*	*Management*
Agree	38 (15.0)	36 (34.0)	12 (10.0)
Disagree	117 (46.1)	54 (51.0)	62 (51.7)
No comment	99 (38.9)	16 (15.0)	46 (38.3)
Total	254	106	120

The data refute the allegation that the syllabus is anti-union. The responses to the above statement corroborated the perceptions of worker-teachers that syllabus is not anti-union. But the sub-committee of the Regional Advisory Committee, Bombay (1967)[13] remarked that the printed syllabus was lacking in trade union orientation. Virmani[14] (1986) commented that only management oriented topics like safety, discipline, productivity were included in the syllabus and the workers started loosing interest in the programme. Quoting worker-teachers, he observed that there is biased emphasis on topics in the syllabus in favour of the party taking initiative. If it is the management, management oriented topics are given prominence, when the initiative is taken by the union topics of trade unionism are given importance.

Table 6.15
Responses to the Statement "Syllabus is Not Relevant"

Responses	*Worker Trainee*	*Union Officials*	*Management*
Agree	162 (63.8)	30 (28.4)	52 (43.4)
Disagree	63 (24.8)	38 (35.8)	27 (22.5)
No comment	29 (11.4)	38 (35.8)	41 (34.1)
Total	254	106	120

The data in the table suggest that majority of worker-trainees (63.8%) endorsed the view that the syllabus is not relevant to the day to day needs of the workers. The union respondents did not fully subscribe to the view that syllabus is irrelevant. But the management supported this view. The worker-teachers also agreed with this statement that syllabus is not relevant.

As mentioned earlier, the syllabus for workers' education programme has been modified from time to time in tune with the development in the organised sector. The government claims that the syllabus is framed on a tripartite basis with appropriate representation to all involved parties. It may be pertinent to quote Virmani's (1986) experience with regard to the seriousness of the member of the syllabus review committee who pleaded ignorance about the syllabus. He commented that the members do not take the review seriously. Ramaswamy[15] (1985) commented that the information imparted in the name of workers' education is hardly in accordance with their every day experiences in the enterprise, trade union and community. According to Ramanujam, veteran trade unionist who later became the chairperson of the central board for workers education, the efforts of the board is to give an integrated education about our country, trade unions, industrial relations including participative management in the organised sector. Also emphasis on the co-operative efforts between labour and management to improve discipline, efficiency and productivity, sacrificing the sectional interest of the workers is laid in the broad interest of the community and nation (Ramanujam[16] 1981). Sarma, A.M.[17] (1980) suggested that syllabus should be made more flexible to suit the needs of different groups of workers in the industry. Syllabus Review Committee[18] (1994) found that the syllabus contains too many topics and are too general. It suggested that the programmes must be more specific and functional and joint educational programme for both workers and management be conducted.

Table 6.16
Responses to the Statement that Study Tour is Main Attraction and Without it the Programme cannot be Sustained

Responses	*Worker Trainee*	*Union Officials*	*Management*
Yes	34 (13.4)	31 (29.2)	64 (53.3)
No	188 (13.4)	20 (18.9)	19 (15.8)
No comment	32 (12.6)	55 (51.9)	37 (30.9)
Total	254	106	120

The responses of worker-trainees to the question exploded the myth that study tour is the only factor that is binding them. An overwhelming majority of them (74.0%) categorically stated 'No' to the question implying that the continuity of the programme is not dependent on perks and facilities. Management respondents persisted with the view that the study tour is driving the workers to enroll themselves for training. The union respondents (51.9%) are non-committal. The data clearly show that study tour and other facilities are not the main factors that entice the worker-trainees to the programme. The worker-teachers who still hold that study tour is the main attraction have not shared the same idea. The study/industrial tour received flak from the trainees. One trainee remarked that the behaviour of the workers in the tour is not good, they are not a disciplined lot. Another observed that the purpose of study tour is defeated as it is converted into 'sight seeing programme'. Some suggested that the behaviour of workers during study tour should be certified by the worker-teacher and disciplinary action be initiated against erring trainees.

Any training programme has its value and the workers' education programme has the objectives of creating awareness and development of leadership qualities among workers. There were studies reporting positive impact of the scheme on the workers. In the light of the positive out comes reported by the earlier studies, improvement in the knowledge levels, productivity etc among workers it has been felt that workers' education be made compulsory. Other workers may reap the advantages of the scheme also. Keeping this in view the respondents were asked to spell out their views on the statement that workers' education be made compulsory to the workers. The responses are presented in the following table.

Table 6.17
Responses to this Statement Workers' Education be Made Compulsory

Responses	*Worker Trainee*	*Union Officials*	*Management*
Agree	65 (25.6)	28 (26.4)	35 (29.2)
Disagree	68 (26.8)	59 (55.7)	61 (50.8)
No comment	121 (47.6)	19 (17.9)	24 (20.0)
Total	254	106	120

From this table it becomes obvious that majority of the respondents from worker-trainees, unions and management did not share with the worker-teachers, the idea of making the scheme, a compulsory one. Worker-trainees, unions and management personnel did not share the perception of the worker-teacher that the scheme be made compulsory to all the workers.

References

1. Sarma, A.M. (1980) *Workers Education Scheme—An Evaluation,* Indian Journal of Social Work, July, No. 2, pp. 123-133.
2. Unnithan Sivapalan, T.R. (1990) *An Enquiry into the Workers Education Programme in Kerala with a View to Suggest Improvements* (unpublished thesis) University of Kerala, p. 180.
3. Virmani, B.R. (1986) *Evaluation of Workers Education* (unpublished report) Administrative Staff College of India, Hyderabad, p. 189.
4. ILO (1984) *The Central Board of Workers Education Celebrates Its 25th Birthday* (under labour education in the world), Labour Education, No. 54, ILO Office, Geneva.
5. CBWE, (1982) *23rd Annual Report of CBWE,* Nagpur, p. 14.
6. Ramaswamy, E.A. (1986) *Towards an Enlightened Workforce Business India,* Dec., p. 42.
7. Pant, S.C. (1973) *Indian Labour Problems,* Chaitanya Publishing House, Allahabad, p. 231.
8. Ramaswamy, E.A. (1985) *What Education do Workers Need?* Indian Journal of Adult Education, Vol. 46, No. 5, May, p. 27.
9. *Ibid.*, p. 28.
10. *Ibid.*, p. 30.
11. Kakkar, N.K. (1973) *Workers Education in India,* Sterling Publications, New Delhi, p. 290.
12. Virmani, B.R. (1986) *Evaluation of Workers Education* (unpublished report) Administrative Staff College of India, Hyderabad, p. 191.
13. CBWE (1967) *Report of the Regional Advisory Committee,* Bombay, WEC.
14. Virmani, B.R. (1986) *Evaluation of Workers Education* (unpublished report) Administrative Staff College of India, Hyderabad, p. 192.
15. Ramaswamy, E.A. (1985) "What Education Do Workers Need", Indian Journal of Adult Education, Vol. 46, No. 5, p. 28.
16. Ramanujam, G. (1981) *Workers Education—New Vistas,* CBWE, Nagpur, p. 27.
17. Sarma, A.M. (1980) *Workers Education Scheme—An Evaluation,* Indian Journal of Social Work, July, No. 2, p. 130.
18. CBWE (1994) *Report of the Syllabus Review Committee on Training Programmes of CBWE,* Nagpur, July, p. 14.

7

The Outcome of the Workers' Education Scheme: Perception of Worker-Teachers, Worker-Trainees, Trade Union Officials and Management Personnel

Introduction

Evaluation is of crucial importance in ascertaining whether or not programme is proving to be effective or its objectives are being achieved. Evaluation of training is defined as "an attempt to obtain information (feedback) on the effects of a training programme, and to assess the value of training in the light of information" (Hamblin[1], 1985). He postulated four levels of evaluations (1) reaction level (2) learning level (3) behavioural level, and (4) organisational level. The last three levels are also referred as immediate, intermediate and ultimate levels and each of these levels of evaluation has been intricately related and forms a casual chain. However, when the objectives of training are already defined, evaluation at a particular level is possible. It is impossible to evaluate at the more distant level. One of the difficulties that prevents a reasonable assessment of the efficacy of training programme is the fact that training is not the only intervention but a number of variables operate and influence the attitude and motivational level of the people. This is over and above the aspect that between the time a training intervention takes place and its impact is registered there is a time lag and corroborating the results with the training programmes becomes difficult (Bharat Wakhlu[2], 1997).

The present workers' education scheme is one of the few attempts made so far in our country to improve the knowledge of rank and file workers about trade unionism, labour-management relations and the like, all of which are responsible for the smooth functioning of organisation and for maintaining industrial peace and growth in the country.

Here an attempt is made to assess the effectiveness of the training programme. The respondents (worker-teacher, trade union official and management personnel) were asked to rate the trained workers they closely know in terms of improvements in the following areas: (1) productivity mindedness (2) awareness of rights and duties (3) discipline consciousness (4) leadership qualities (5) worker-management relationship. Worker-trainee was asked to self-appraise in the above areas. The answers to the questions are arranged in a three-point scale: *(a)* Improvement *(b)* No improvement *(c)* can not say.

Productivity

Productivity means the ability to produce or efficiency especially in industry measured by comparing the amount produced (output) with the time taken or the resources (input) used to produce it. Productivity is the quantity or volume of the major product or service that an organisation produces (Stephen P. Robins[3], 1994). In other words, it is the amount of work that is being produced in the organisation in terms of how much and how well. High productivity is what makes an organisation thrive. In general productivity can be considered as related to efficiency. Broadly it is a relation between output and input single or combination of few or all. Productivity is controlled by human and non-human variables. Among the human, social and individual and the non-human variables include machines, raw materials, finance and energy. Finally productivity is contingent on an employees motivation. The best trained employee one who not only has the ability but has access to the most advanced piece of equipment will not be productive if he or she is unwilling to be so. Attitude plays an important role as to whether an employee has the propensity to work. The component of productivity education would go a long way in awareness building, creating positive attitude among the work force on productivity. The respondents were asked whether they have observed any change in the productivity awareness or productivity mindedness among trained workers. The responses are presented below.

Table 7.1
Showing Perception of Respondents with Regard to Improvements in Productivity Mindedness

Responses	*Worker Teachers*	*Worker Trainees*	*Union Officials*	*Management Personnel*
Improvement	72 (53.7)	98 (38.6)	59 (55.7)	26 (21.7)
No improvement	29 (21.6)	39 (15.3)	20 (18.9)	66 (55.0)
Can not say	33 (24.7)	117 (46.1)	27 (25.4)	28 (23.4)
Total	134	254	106	120

The data in the table reveal that majority of (53.7%) worker-teacher and union officials (55.7%) perceived improvement in the workers while the self-appraisal made by the trainees show that a large number (46.1%) did not say anything. Management respondents differed in their perception. While majority (55.7%) of the trade union respondents found improvement in the productivity mindedness among workers, their management personnel (55%) do not share the same perception. The results are in consonance with their conflicting views on different aspects. The results of the data reveal that with the exception of management personnel, there has been an agreement among other category of respondents that training in workers' education brought some change in their attitude towards productivity. This is in line with the observation of J.S. Sodhi[4] (1997) that with the opening up of our economy in the nineties, there is some awareness among workers and unions for the need to improve efficiency and productivity.

Bandopadhyay[5] (1977), Rizvi and Khan[6] (1984) reported improvement in the productivity consciousness among workers after undergoing training in workers' education, while Indian National Trade Union Congress's Committee felt that the impact of workers' education programme on productivity was not discernable even where even a majority of the workers attended the programme (1965)[7]. CBWE in its diagnostic studies attributed the lack of impact of the programme on productivity to lesser importance given for productivity in the workers' education programme itself (1969)[8].

General Awareness About Rights and Duties

One of the stated objectives of workers' education is to equip workers for intelligent participation in the social and economic development of the nation for understanding of their rights and obligations as citizens as workers in industry as members and officials of their trade unions. Creating awareness among workers regarding their duties along with their requisite knowledge of law will equip the workers with the necessary confidence to participate meaningfully in all spheres of his activity. It also creates conducive atmosphere for industrial peace, reducing the possibilities of strikes and work stoppages (Sodhi[9] 1997).

Table 7.2

Perception of Respondents with Regard to Improvement in General Awareness About Rights and Duties

Responses	*Worker Teachers*	*Worker Trainees*	*Union Officials*	*Management Personnel*
Improvement	102 (76.1)	130 (51.2)	67 (63.2)	68 (56.7)
No improvement	25 (18.7)	55 (21.6)	11 (10.4)	32 (26.7)
Can not say	7 (5.2)	69 (27.2)	28 (26.4)	20 (16.7)
Total	134	254	106	120

The results of data show that there was significant agreement in the views of the parties to the worker education programme. There has been agreement or similarity of views with regard to the improvement in the awareness about rights and duties. But the management personnel differentiated between rights and duties. While they agreed that there has been improvement with regard to their awareness about their rights what they found visibly among workers is more awareness about their rights rather than their duties.

Majority of the earlier studies (Bandopadhyay[10], 1977; Sarma, A.M.[11] 1980; Rizvi and Khan[12]; Unnithan[13] 1990) found improvement in the general awareness among workers about their rights, there has been criticism that workers' education failed to make the workers responsible by imparting the responsibilities and duties of workers toward the industry and the nation. Admitting the fact, the former chairman of the workers' education observed that education by the board has so far laid greater emphasis on the rights of the workman and trade unions. There were of course references to the responsibilities of workers. But that was only nominal. The result is that there has been lopsided development more about their rights than their responsibilities (Ramanujam[14] 1981).

Leadership Qualities

Development of leadership qualities in the rank and file of the workers and to promote the growth of democratic process in the organisation is one of the objectives of workers' education.

Leadership is defined "as the process of influencing the activities of an individual or a group in efforts toward goal achievement in a given situation. In essence, leadership involves accomplishing goals with and through people" (Paul H. and K.H. Blenchard[15], 1974). In the analysis of leadership qualities several models have been formulated such as traits theories, behaviour theories, path-goal theory and leader participation model (David and Robins[16], 1994) while trait theories postulate certain traits which may be present in certain individuals who set them apart as leaders from non-leaders, the behaviourist approach seeks to find critical behavioural determinants of leadership. Such an assumption would lead to designing programmes for effective leadership. The contingency models hinge on situational analysis and path-goal model seeks to emphasize leaders' ability to assist followers in attaining their goal. Participation in decision-making powers is emphasized by the leader participation model.

The trade union movement in India started with an outsider as the mentor and this position continued for varied reasons (Siqueira[17], 1994). According to him the reasons for continuance of outsiders are the fear of victimization, lack of knowledge of law, need for political connections. There are also studies which reported steady decline of outsiders in the leadership positions and the emergence of local plant level unions leadership. Punekar[18] (1958), Madhusudhana Rao[19] (1986), Sarje Rao and Salunkha[20] (1994) in their studies found that outsiders are on decline. Sarjerao, A. and Salunkha found twelve out of 17 leaders in their study were reported to have undergone training under the workers' education programme. The respondents were asked whether the training in workers' education resulted in the development of leadership qualities.

Table 7.3
Development of Leadership

Responses	*Worker Teachers*	*Worker Trainees*	*Union Officials*	*Management Personnel*
Improvement	77 (57.5)	130 (51.2)	68 (64.1)	47 (39.2)
No improvement	39 (29.1)	100 (39.4)	16 (15.1)	55 (45.8)
Can not say	18 (13.4)	24 (9.4)	22 (20.8)	18 (15.0)
Total	134 (100.0)	254 (100.0)	18 (15.0)	120 (100.0)

Developing leadership among the workers is one of the objectives of the workers' education programme, but not the sole one. The board is conducting separate leadership training courses to the workers. Majority of the studies concentrated on leadership, enquiring whether training at unit level classes resulted in the promotion of leadership qualities in the workers. The present study also sought to make this aspect clear.

The data in the table show that majority (57.5%) of the worker-teachers, and trained workers reported (51.2%) improvement in the leadership qualities after undergoing training. The responses of the management and trade union representatives differed considerably with regard to their perception on the development of leadership qualities. While the trade union respondents held positive views (64.1% reported improvement in leadership qualities), management did not find any change in the leadership qualities.

The worker-teachers and worker-trainees were further inquired whether they held any post in the union or any other body in the industry after undergoing training in workers' education training. The data are presented in the following table.

Table 7.4
Did You Hold Any Post After Undergoing Training?

Responses	*Worker Teacher*	*Trainee Worker*
Yes	78 (58.2)	52 (20.5)
No	56 (41.8)	202 (79.5)
Total	134 (100.0)	254 (100.0)

The data show that a majority (58.2%) of the respondents among worker teachers reported that they held some posts after the training like becoming works committee member, member of the bipartite committees etc. In the case of workers trained in the unit level class, the picture is not encouraging. Out of the 254 worker-trainees respondents who underwent training in unit level classes hardly 20 per cent of them held positions after training. A thorough perusal of the posts held by them suggest that majority of them held positions, or became members of the numerous bipartite committees that operate in the industrial organisations, and an insignificant percentage of the respondents occupied positions in the union hierarchy.

Table 7.5
Nature of the Posts Held by Respondents

Posts	*Worker Teacher*	*Worker Trainee*
Member of the Works Committees	28 (35.9)	12 (23.1)
Other Bipartite Committees	36 (46.2)	34 (65.4)
Member of the union executive	14 (17.9)	6 (11.5)
Total	78 (100.0)	52 (100.0)

The data suggest that ascending the union hierarchy or occupying positions in the trade union movement is difficult. The data may give credence to the belief that most of the trade union leaders develop vested interest in their positions and nurture misgiving in genuine development of leadership qualities among the rank and file workers.

Devaki Devi[21] (1983), Sivapalan Unnithan[22] (1990), Mukherjee[23] (1985), suggested that worker-teachers rose to the higher positions in the trade union after their exposure and involvement in training. Monthly publication of the CBWE 'Workers' education' invariably carries success stories suggesting that former worker teachers reached higher positions in the union or other fields. The workers' education board claims credit for their ascendancy. A close examination of the workers who rose to the higher positions, quoted by the earlier studies, reveal the fact that they are all worker-teachers, not the workers trained in the unit level classes. The position of workers who have undergone training in the unit level classes has not been probed or thoroughly investigated. The trade union sends active trade unionists to undergo worker-teacher training course so the pre-training position of worker is an important determinant to be considered while attributing the success to the training programme. In this context the observations of the trade unions before the labour commission is pertinent to mention. The Committee on Workers' Education of National Commission on Labour observed that "most of the unions did not feel that the worker-teachers who returned to do union work have not improved their capacity as a result of training (1967)[24]. Report of the sub-committee of the Regional

Advisory Committee (1967)[25] state that all the unions have agreed that worker-teachers do not acquire necessary skills for organising the workers and therefore do not become better trade unionists.

Labour-Management Relations

Good labour-management relations is a sine-qua-non for rapid industrialisation and quick economic progress of our country. The problem of labour-management relations gained importance in the context of harnessing all the energies and resources of the country for the successful implementation of the five year plans with a democratic set up. "Labour-management relations is the composite result of attitudes and approaches of the employers and worker towards each other with regard to planning supervision, direction and coordination of the activities of an organisation with the minimum of human effort and function with an animating spirit of cooperation and with proper regard for the genuine well-being of all members of the organisation" (Tead and Metcalfe[26], 1990). It is generally treated as the relations conducted by the strong and independent associations of employers and trade unions. Of late, the importance of healthy industrial relations and the maintenance of industrial peace for raising the tempo of productivity has assumed significance in the context of globalised economic policies, competitiveness in maintaining quality. The primary function is to promote good congruence between capital and labour. The political environment, business cycles and the ideological bent of the trade union leadership influence them. In India there has been sharp decline in intensity, frequency and severity of industrial disputes since 1987 (Ajit Mathur[27], 1994) and the tenor of the trade unions which was militant has become less strident.

The workers' education programme aims at maintaining industrial peace and harmony and the syllabus of the three-tier workers' education programe includes topics like industrial relations and trade unions movement. This aspect has also been covered by the present study. The respondents were asked whether the training resulted in improved labour-management relations consciousness.

Table 7.6
Perception of Respondents with Regard to Improvement in LMR Consciousness

Respondents	*Worker Teachers*	*Worker Trainees*	*Union Officials*	*Management Personnel*
Improvement	87 (64.9)	153 (60.2)	58 (54.7)	28 (23.4)
No improvement	27 (20.2)	70 (27.6)	19 (17.9)	54 (45.0)
Can not say	20 (14.9)	31 (12.2)	29 (27.4)	38 (31.6)
Total	134 (100.0)	254 (100.0)	106 (100.0)	120 (100.0)

The data show that majority of the worker-teachers and trainees found there has been improvement in the labour-managmeent relations indicating that the disputes with the managements have come down, work stoppages have been averted or they were not the parties to the disputes, and managements held the view that there was no change in them after undergoing training.

Discipline Consciousness

Discipline or orderly behaviour is essential for attaining the organisational objectives. Discipline sets a pattern of acceptable behaviour and performance on the part of human beings. According to Earl R. Bram Blett[28] (1969) "Discipline in the broad sense means—the opposite view of confusion. It is a fundamental requirement for the people working in a plant just as it is for other segments of society. Shop discipline as we use the term, doe snot mean strict and technical observance of rigid rules and regulations. It simply means working, cooperating and behaving in a normal and orderly way, as any reasonable person would expect an employee to do (1961). According to Pfiffner[29] (1955) discipline is synomously used with morale. As used in this sense the term undoubtedly mean "the manner in which the members of an organisation conform to the established rules and regulations that set the norms of operation". As Mooney[30] (1947) observes "when labour and boss are bound by the same common understanding of some common purpose, the discipline is an plan that no other form can reach".

According to Ramanujam[31] (1981) the objectives of workers' education scheme lays increasing emphasis on the need for cooperative efforts between labour and management to improve discipline, efficiency and productivity, on the obligations and responsibilities of workers and new objectives sensitise the workers more to their obligations towards the community rather than training in methods for achieving their sectional ends.

It has been felt necessary to find out whether the training in workers' education resulted in discipline consciousness among workers. The responses of the worker-teachers, trainees, untrained workers, unions and management are presented below.

Table 7.7
Perception of Respondents with Regard to Improvement in Discipline Consciousness

Respondents	*Worker Teachers*	*Worker Trainees*	*Union Officials*	*Management Personnel*
Improvement	80 (59.7)	182 (17.6)	45 (37.5)	18 (17.0)
No improvement	34 (25.4)	18 (7.1)	50 (41.6)	52 (49.0)
Can not say	20 (14.9)	54 (21.3)	25 (20.9)	36 (34.0)
Total	134 (100.0)	254 (100.0)	120 (100.0)	106 (100.0)

The data on discipline consciousness suggest that while worker-teachers and trained workers found improvement in discipline consciousness, unions and management personnel do not share the same view. Rizvi and Khan[32] (1984) study found the training in workers' education improved discipline consciousness, while Sivapalan Unnithan[33] (1990) concluded that the managements felt that the programme resulted in indiscipline and negative attitude towards the industry.

Summary

An overview of the results of the data presented in the preceding pages revealed that majority of the worker-teachers, union officials and worker-trainees found improvement in the productivity mindedness. Management personnel who found no improvement in the productivity mindedness did not share this perception. With regard to the improvements in the awareness about rights and duties, majority of the respondents of all categories was in agreement that there was some improvement in the awareness about rights and duties. In the case of development of leadership qualities, there has been unanimity among worker-teachers trainees and union officials that there has been some improvement in the leadership qualities while management personnel did not subscribe to this view. Worker-teachers, trainees, union officials found improvement in the labour management relations after training while the management personnel did not share this positive outcome. With regard to discipline consciousness worker-teachers and worker-trainees are in agreement that there is improvement in discipline consciousness while management and unions do not share the same view.

References

1. Hamblin (1985) *An Introductory Course on Teaching and Training Methods for Management Development*, Sterling Publishers, New Delhi.
2. Bharat Wakhlu (1997) *Effective Approaches for Training and Development*, Personnel Today, NIPM Publication, Calcutta, April-June, Vol. XVIII, No. 1, pp. 17-21.
3. Stephen, Robins (1994) *Essentials of Organisational Behaviour*, Prentice Hall of India, New Delhi.
4. Sodhi, J.S. (1997) *Issues, Trends and Developments in Industrial Relations in India and Other South Asian Countries*, Indian Journal of Industrial Relations, Vol. 32, No. 4, April, pp. 368-369.
5 Bandopadhyay, Swaraj, I. (1977) *Impact of Workers Education—A Case Study*, Workers Education, CBWE, Nagpur.
6. Rizvi, P.H. and Khan, M.A. (1984) *UGC Research Project on Impact of Workers Education*, Workers Education, June, pp. 18-20.
7. INTUC (1965) *Labour Policies and Programmes in the Fourth Five Year Plan*, Chapter II, New Delhi, INTUC Publication, 49.

8. CBWE (1969) *Diagnostic Studies*, CBWE, Nagpur.
9. Sodhi, J.S. (1997) *Issues, Trends and Developments in Industrial Relations in India and Other South Asian Countries*, Indian Journal of Industrial Relations, Vol. 32, No. 4, April, pp. 368-369.
10. Bandopadhyay, Swaraj, I. (1977) *Impact of workers Education—A Case Study*, Workers Education, CBWE, Nagpur.
11. Sarma, A.M. (1989) *Workers Education Scheme—An Evaluation*, Indian Journal of Social Work, Vol. XLI, July, No. 2, pp. 123-133.
12. Bandopadhyay, Swaraj I. (1977) *Impact of Workers Education—A Case Study*, Workers Education, CBWE, Nagpur.
13. Unnithan Sivapalan, T.R. (1990) *An Inquiry Into the Workers Education Programme in Kerala with a View to Suggest Improvements*, University of Kerala (Unpublished Doctoral Dissertation), p. 102.
14. Ramanujam, G. (1981) *Workers' Education—New Vistas*, CBWE, Nagpur.
15. Paul, H., K.H. Blenchard (1974) *Management of Organisational Behaviour*.
16. David A. Cecenzo, Stephen P. Robins (1994) *Personnel/Human Resource Management*, Prentice Hall of India, New Delhi.
17. Siqueira, V. (1994) *Industrial Relations: Opportunities in the Mid-nineties*, Indian Journal of Industrial Relations, Vol. LV, No. 2, April, pp. 256-260.
18. Punekar, S.D. (1958) *Outside Leadership of Trade Unions—A Bombay Survey*, Economic Weekly, Vol. 10, July, pp. 877-879.
19. Madhusudhana Rao, M. (1986) *Labour Management Relations and Trade Unions Leadership: A Behavioural Study of Union Leaders*, Deep & Deep Publications, New Delhi, p. 150.
20. Sarje Rao, A., Salunkha (1994) *Emerging Trade Unions Leadership*, Indian Journal of Industrial Relations, Vol. 29, No. 3, Jan.
21. Devaki Devi, P. (1983) *Worker Teachers Lead the Trade Unions: Impact of Workers Education*, April, CBWE, Nagpur, pp. 24-26.
22. Unnithan Sivapalan, T.R. (1990) *An Inquiry Into the Workers Education Programme in Kerala with a View to Suggest Improvements*, University of Kerala (Unpublished Doctoral Dissertation), p. 105.
23. Mukherjee (1985) *Workers Education in India—Some*

Recollections, Workshop on Workers Education in India, Organised by the Administrative Staff College of India, Hyderabad.

25. CBWE (1967) *A Report of the Regional Advisory Committee on Workers' Education*, Bombay.
26. Tead & Metcalf (1990) *Personnel Administration*, quoted in B.P. Singh's Personnel Management and Industrial Relations, Damport Roy & Sons, New Delhi.
27. Ajit Mathur (1994) *The Future of Trade Unions*, Indian Journal of Social Work, LV, No. 2, April.
28. Earl R. Bran Blett (1961) *Maintenance of Discipline*, Management of Personnel Quarterly, Vol. 1, No. 1, Aulumm, p. 10.
29. John M. Pfiffner (1955) *The Supervision of Personnel Human Relations in the Management of Man*, Prentice Hall Inc., New York, pp. 345-363.
30. Moomey, J.O. (1947) *The Principles of Organisation*, Harper & Row Publishing Inc., New York.
31. Ramanujam, G. (1981) *Workers' Education—New Vistas*, CBWE, Nagpur.
32. Bandopadhyay, Swaraj, I. (1977) *Impact of Workers Education—A Case Study*, Workers Education, CBWE, Nagpur.
33. Unnithan Sivapalan, T.R. (1990) *An Inquiry Into the Workers Education Programme in Kerala with a View to Suggest Improvements*, University of Kerala (Unpublished Doctoral Dissertation), p. 110.

8

Conclusions and Suggestions

Several scholars from different disciplines have researched the Scheme of Workers' Education. A significant drawback of all these studies is that they did not focus on the relevance and adequacy of the syllabus and examine their congruence with the aims of the scheme. The training component of the Workers' Education Scheme did not figure in any of the studies. All these studies concentrated on worker-trainees and their perception of the impact, thus neglecting the worker-teacher who shoulders the responsibility of conducting unit level classes and imparting education to the workers. The progress, whatever, made by the board is largely attributed the efforts of the worker-teachers. It is against this background that the present study of workers' education makes an attempt to fill the gap in the existing literature on this subject.

As the existing studies were limited in focus, aims, methods, the universe and sample, the researcher tried to make the study more broad based covering a large sample of worker-teachers and other functionaries concerned with the scheme. The present study elicited views from 134 worker-teachers, 254 worker-trainees, 120 management personnel and 106 trade union officials. This chapter presents the main conclusions based on the analysis of data discussed in the preceding chapters.

Profile of the Respondents

Age

Majority of the respondents (54.5%) were in the age group of 31-40 years. The ages of the worker-teacher respondents range from 20 to 48 years while the mean age was found to be approximately 35 years. It can be concluded that the middle-aged workers are more likely to evince interest on workers education. Sarma A.M. (1980) Unnithan (1990) studies corroborated these findings. Kakkar[1] (1973) does not support the same. He found young workers (20-30 years) constituted majority of the worker-teachers (52%). The wide difference in the ages of the workers teachers has to be understood in terms of time lag between the two studies. Kakkar's study was undertaken in the first decade of launching of the programme and it is natural that the euphoria associated with the scheme lured the young workers to the programme. The present study was undertaken after 40 years of its existence, there was less steam left out in the scheme, hence could not attract young workers. The fact that 41 years and above age group respondents formed 20 per cent of the sample is in consonance with the (Hasley Frazis[2], 2000) finding that age after certain stage reduces the incentive to train.

A large number (45.6%) of the worker-trainees belonged to 41 years above age group. The presence of large number of older workers among the trainees negates the theory (Hasley Frazis *et al.* 2000) that the older workers were less likely to receive training and the finding goes to prove that for learning age is not a hindrance and learning is a continuous process. Compared to the worker-teachers, the worker-trainees are relatively older.

Majority of the trade union leaders and management personnel also belonged to the same category of above 41 years age group.

Religion

An overwhelming majority of the worker-teachers, trainees, union officials and management personnel belong to Hindu religion. This is in tune with the religious composition of the nation.

Sex

All the worker-teachers are males. In case of worker-trainees an overwhelming (97.6%) respondents are males. Females constituted (2.4%) an insignificant percentage of the worker-trainees. This has been in tune with the finding that women are less likely to receive training (Venum[3] 1995). The Central Board of Workers Education has been criticized on this count and board is making special efforts to rope women into the programme. Worker-teacher training programmes exclusively for women have been organised by the board. Despite this, the number of women workers getting trained in the unit level classes is abysmally negligible. This may be due to the inconvenient timings of the unit level classes which dissuade women worker from the programme.

In case of trade union officials and management personnel almost all of them are men (100.0 per cent among trade union officials, 97.5 per cent among management personnel).

Caste

Backward caste workers constituted majority (50.8%) among worker-teachers and single largest group (47%) among worker-trainees. Among trade union officials also, backward classes constituted majority (54.7%), while forward caste people formed 56.7 per cent of the management personnel.

It is interesting to find backward classes (considered to be socially and educationally backward) respondents are evincing interest to receive training in workers education. This may be due their inclination to compensate the loss of schooling/college.

Education

Majority (68.0%) of the worker-teachers have SSC and above qualifications and it can be said that the sample consists of a considerable number of fairly educated persons.

The fact that Bachelor degree holders constituted insignificant number contradicts the theory (Brown 1989; Lillard and Tan 1986; Lynch, 1992; Lynch and Black 1998) that more educated receive more training. When the benefits of training in terms of hike in wages, career growth, are more, there is likelihood that better educated persons incline to receive more off-the job training. The reason for less involvement of better educated workers in the worker-teachers training programme may be due to the fact that training in worker education do not guarantee or bring any returns to them. The analysis of the data on the educational attainments suggest that (68.0% of the worker-teachers) had matric and above qualification, there is a substantial improvement in terms of the educational attainments of the worker-teachers compared to the educational attainments of Kakkar's (1973) study. He reported 72.0 per cent of them had less than matriculation qualification. The improvement in the educational attainments of worker-teachers is in tune with the increase in literacy rate of the country that stands at 52.2 per cent (Census, 1991).

Educational attainments of the worker-trainees revealed that a large number of workers had (41.7%) matriculation/ SSC as qualification. The fact that large number of lesser-educated workers preferring to receive training disproves the theory that lesser educated are less likely to receive training.

The data show that the worker-trainees are relatively lesser educated than the worker-teachers.

Educational attainments of the trade union officials and management personnel suggest that majority of the trade union official had intermediate qualification (58.5%) while three-fourths of the management personnel had bachelor degree and above qualification. The difference in the educational attachments may be attributed to the fact that bachelors degree is a minimum qualification, for entry into managerial job, while no such qualification is required for occupying leadership position in the union.

Experience

A large percentage (47%) of the workers had 9 to 16 year of experience. On an average, work experience of the respondents is 12.3 years. It may be inferred from the data that experienced workers are more likely to be interested in improving their knowledge and imparting it to their brethren. The finding that respondents with 17 to 24 years of experience constituted nearly one-fourth of the sample corroborates with the theory that suggests that interest in training decreases with increase in tenure of service (Harley Frazis *et. al.* 2000).

Nearly two-thirds (64.5%) of the worker-trainees had 11-20 years of experience. Both worker-teachers and trainees are senior people. Among trade unions officials 94 per cent of them are employees (insiders) and outsiders constituted 6 per cent of the sample. A large number of trade union officials had less than 10 years of experience, while two-thirds of management personnel had 11-20 year of experience.

Type of Job

More than three-fourths (76.9%) of the respondents among worker-teachers, and 80 per cent of the trainees were holding blue-collar jobs. This suggests that blue-collar workers are more likely to receive training in non-technical aspects of the job and industry as their knowledge level of the above is considerably low. White collar workers with better education is less likely to be attracted to worker-teacher training, as their familiarity with the subject or content of the programme in the college/formal schooling dissuade them from the programme.

Union Affiliation

Union affiliation pattern of the workers suggests that majority of them (55.2%) are from centrist unions. In India the INTUC, the labour wing of the Indian National Congress, is the leading centrist union. The dominance of workers belonging to centrist unions, particularly INTUC in the workers education programme may be due its efforts to lend support to the programme launched by its parent political party, the Indian National Congress. Since it is a government sponsored programme the INTUC which is the labour wing of the Congress Party, the dominant ruling party for 45 out of 50 years of the country's independence took advantage, sponsored more members for the programme. Majority of worker-trainees (58.3%) and trade union officials (58.3%) belonged to centrist unions.

Scheme of Workers' Education: Worker-Teachers Perceptions

Selection Procedure

Unions played a key role in the selection process as majority (59%) of the respondents were of the view that their unions selected them for the training programme. This finding has been coroborrated by Virmani (1986).

This is in conformity with the selection procedure evolved by the board which gives free hand to the unions in the selection of workers for the worker-teacher training. The management takes initiative only when the unions do not come forward with the names or when workers request the intervention of the management. Since it is a government sponsored programme, most of the industries that nominate workers are government owned public sector organisations, the managements play a passive role in the selection procedure.

Criteria

A large number (64.1%) of the worker-teachers felt that their active participation in union promoted the prospects of their selection to the worker-teacher training.

One of the criteria the unions follow while nominating the workers is active participation in union activities. This may jeopardize the chances of workers who show genuine interest in the programme, but remain inactive in the trade unions. This method of selection gives lot of leverage to the unions, which use it as reward to the loyal members. This type of criticism is often heard in the union circles. According to Virmani union participation is the main criterion in selecting the worker-teachers and not based on criteria of being a good teacher (1986).

Reasons for Joining the Programme

Majority of the respondents (63.4%) of them said that they have undergone training to gain knowledge. Gaining and imparting of knowledge is the motive for undergoing three months intensive coaching at the regional centre.

Syllabus

The views of the respondents on the adequacy of time allotted to cover the syllabus have been elicited and the conclusions are presented below.

Know Your Country

An analysis of the responses to the item in the syllabus 'know your country' to which 20 hours of teaching are allotted, a large number of (47.0%) the respondents felt the time allotted to this item is much. It is observed that the topic 'know your country' is not well received by younger respondents when compared to middle aged respondents. The responses were cross-tabulated with the level of education of the respondents. It was found that a less educated worker-teacher is less likely to favour teaching of subjects like 'know your country' than higher educated respondents. With regard to the nature of job it was found that technical job holders are less likely to favour this item in the syllabus than the non-technical jobholders.

Know Your Industry

To another item in the syllabus 'know your industry' eight hours of teaching are allotted. An overwhelming majority of the respondents (90.0%) expressed the view that the time allotted is more than what is necessary.

Productivity Education

Reacting to the time allotted to cover the topic 'productivity' majority of the (53.0%) respondents felt that the teaching hours allotted to it is in excess. It is found that productivity education has not been well received by the worker-teachers as it is seen as a management oriented subject. Analysis of the data on productivity by age of the respondents revealed that there is an association between these two variables. It was observed that respondents in lower as well as higher age groups were less disposed towards productivity education, compared to the middle aged.

Industrial Relations

The topic 'Industrial Relations' is allotted 11 hours. Analysis of data show that a good number (38.1%) of the respondents felt that the hours allotted to it is just right.

And an equal percentage of them wanted more time to be given to this item. This may be due to the subject matter that includes grievance procedure, collective barraging, strikes and lock-out which sustain their interest. For ambitious workers who want, to occupy leadership position in a union, knowledge of industry relations is a must.

Trade Union Movement

The topic 'trade union movement' has been given special importance in this scheme earmarking 20 hours. Majority (51.5%) of the workers was of the view that the hours allotted to trade union movement are more than what is required.

The items in the syllabus like know your country and know your industry and trade union movement are time consuming exercises as they are not helpful to the workers in their day to day activities, hence they are not palatable. The worker is less inclined towards histories and ideologies of unions, but more towards their mundane bread and butter problems (Holmstrom, 1985).

Labour Economics

The chapter on labour economics is allotted 16 hours. The opinions of the respondents were analysed. The responses to this item revealed that a large number (43%) of the respondents were of the opinion that time allotted to this item is inadequate and as it is the topic of their interest, they wanted more discussion or deliberations on this subject.

Workers Participation Management

An analysis of the opinions on the time allotted to the item "Workers' Participation in Management", majority (56.7%) of workers opined that the teaching hours are inadequate as it is the topic that interests most.

Public Sector

Majority (53.5%) of respondents expressed that the time allotted for topics like 'public sector' is more than what is required. This may be due to their familiarity with the various facets of public sector.

Population Education and Family Welfare

Majority of the respondents (55.3%) reported that number of hours allotted to this item is more than what is required. The workers are more familiar with population education and family welfare as the print and electronic media give wide publicity to the government policy in this regard. Hence they wanted less number of hours be given to this item.

Communication Techniques

On the topic 'Communication Techniques' the analysis of responses revealed that majority of them were of the view that the time allotted to it is in excess of the requirement. This may be due to the over emphasis given in the regional centre on the theoretical aspects like learning process, motivation etc. which are considered as too obtuse for easy comprehension.

Labour Legislation

An overwhelming majority of the respondents (73.9%) were of the view that the time allotted to an interesting topic like 'Important Labour Legislations' is inadequate. This may be due to the fact that the knowledge of law helps the workers in the assertion of their rights vis-a-vis management and gaining acceptance among workers.

Training

The views of the respondents on the adequacy of the duration, coverage of syllabus, level of inputs and their involvement in training etc. were elicited and the present conclusions are based on the analysis of the data presented in the preceding sections.

Duration of Training

The study collected the responses of the worker-teachers on the question whether the period of training was adequate? It was found that majority of the respondents (around 54%) were of the view that the present period of training is not sufficient. Further analysis of the data showed that the majority (75.8%) of the young worker-teacher felt that duration of the training was insufficient when compared with the responses of the middle aged workers. Majority (61.2%) of the blue collared workers, felt that the period is not sufficient. Surprisingly, it was found that the work experience is found to have no bearing on the perception of respondents towards duration of the training programme.

It was also found less educated considered the duration inadequate. This finding runs contrary to overall results on syllabus and the time allotted to it. It is pertinent to note that workers who found the time allotted to majority of the items in the syllabus is more than what is required, felt the duration of training should be increased. They are of the view that some new and important items should be allotted more time and the time given to less important subjects be reduced.

Coverage

A large number of respondents (38.1%) reported that the coverage of the syllabus is poor. Age-wise analysis of the data revealed that a large number (42.5%) of young respondents evaluated the coverage of the syllabus as outstanding. It was found that an overwhelming majority of educated respondents (86.4%) found the coverage of the syllabus poor.

It can be noted that the white collar workers with their relatively higher educational background, have poor opinion on the coverage of the topics in the syllabus.

It was found that lack of systematic coverage of the topics is the general complaint among the worker-teachers. Due to lack of depth in the coverage of syllabus it could not make any headway in achieving the objectives of the programme. Virmani (1986) observed that focus and time allotted to a topic might be on paper only, the coverage being different in practice. Syllabus is not taken seriously and anything could be covered under the specified title. On the other hand extension of syllabus with a view for in depth study may prolong consumption of time which is too precious for the management as man hours are lost due to the deputation of worker.

Level of Inputs

It was found that a large number (44.0%) of the respondent had a feeling that the level of inputs is advanced. It was also found that the two variables namely respondents' age and their attitude towards level of inputs are significantly associated. Majority of the young respondents (66.7%) found that level of inputs advanced while older respondents found the level of inputs as just right. It is observed that majority of (60.5%) less educated respondents found the level of inputs as 'advanced', while respondents with higher educational background found the inputs as elementary.

The analysis revealed that in the opinion of technical jobholders the level of inputs was advanced whereas, for the non-technical jobholders, the level of inputs was elementary. It is interesting to note that there is no significant association between the experience and the level of inputs. White collar workers and other respondents with better education feel that the level of inputs is poor as they have exposure to the subjects either at the college level or in the work place. In contrast respondents with lower education feel that the topics taught in the class are of advanced nature.

Training Methodology

An analysis of the views on the training methodology showed that a majority (55.2%) of the respondents felt that the training methodology (teaching aids, etc.) used in the training programme was poor. This may be due to the fact that over emphasis is given to the traditional method of lecture instead of participatory methods, which helps the learner to retain what has been taught. It was found that majority of the respondents in all the age groups have expressed similar opinion regarding the training methodology. Data also revealed that there is no association between type of job and views on training methodology.

Reading Material

Regarding reading materials supplied by the board during the training programme, a large percentage (42.5%) of the respondents felt that the material is more. Further analysis of the data revealed that there is no association between education background, work experience and age and their attitude towards quantity of training material.

Reading Material (Quality)

Regarding the quality of material, nearly 70 per cent of the respondents rated the material as good or outstanding. Further analysis showed that higher the educational attainments of the respondents lower the rating to the quality of training material. It was also found that an overwhelming majority (76.9%) of the respondents in blue-collar jobs opined that the material supplied to them was of good quality. The data further revealed that there is no association between respondents' experience and attitude towards quality of material supplied.

The Central Board for Workers Education brought about many monographs on different aspects of the syllabus in the regional languages and English that have been found useful to them.

Trainee Involvement

Data on the involvement of trainees in the training programme reveal that a large of them (45.5%) rated their involvement as poor. It was observed that respondents in the lower age group (66.7%) had poor involvement while higher age group respondents had active involvement in the training programme. Further analysis revealed that the involvement of the trainee is dependent on the educational attainments of the respondents. It was found lesser educated respondents (58.1% below SSC, and 60.4% of the SSC respondents) rated their involvement was poor compared to higher educated respondents who rated their involvement good to outstanding. It was also revealed that white-collar workers' involvement in the programmes is more than the blue-collar workers. Analysis of the data relating to 'experience' and 'trainees involvement' revealed that there is an association between these two variables.

Communication

Regarding the communication used in the training programme a large number (38.8%) of the respondents opined that the type of communication used in the programme was good. Further analysis showed that there is no association between age and communication. It is also observed that respondents having higher level of education had rated the communication poor. The results of statistical test revealed that there is an association between the respondents' qualification and their attitude towards communication.

It is also noticed that non-technical jobholders found the communication poor. The level of education and the nature of job have bearing on the perception of workers with regard to the level of communication used in the training course. Poor communication on the part of the teacher, how good the subject may be hinders the learning process.

Unit Level Classes

The workers after undergoing training as worker-teachers in the regional centre are expected to conduct unit level classes for all the workers of the unit. Unit level classes can be conducted in two ways (1) Part time unit level classes of one hour duration after working hours for a period of three months (2) Full time unit level classes for period of three weeks. The study inquired whether the workers are undertaking unit level classes or not. It has been found that an overwhelming majority (84.3%) of the worker-teachers were not taking classes at the time of collection of the data. The reasons for not conducting unit level classes were probed and it was found that non-cooperation of management (33.6%) and non-cooperation of the union (26.9%) were the two main reasons responsible for not conducting unit level classes.

Data on the number of unit level classes taken by the respondents during the period under study revealed that majority of respondents took 1-2 classes (54.5%) and the maximum number of batches trained is 10 and the average came to 2.5.

The selection of workers to the unit level classes is generally left to the worker-teacher and the data on the criteria they followed in selecting worker for the class revealed that nearly half of the respondents reported that they take the worker who evinces interest or who comes forward voluntarily to undergo training.

It is interesting to note that the management of public sector organisation conducts unit level classes in the months of February and March, when the industrial activity is in full swing and financial year closes by March 31. Further probing of this fact revealed that the workers whose presence in the unit hampers production, are sent for ULC and later on study tour to keep them away from the work place. The unit level classes come handy for the management.

A little over 40 per cent of the respondents said that workers join the scheme to gain knowledge. The study revealed that majority of (67.2%) of the respondents were not satisfied with honorarium, which stands at Rs. 100/- and the majority of the worker-teacher (57.8%) wanted the honorarium to be around 201-250.

A majority of the worker-teachers were of the opinion that the present syllabus for the ULC is not sufficient (52.2%). It is also found that majority of the worker-teachers wanted the present duration of the training to be increased, as it is too short a period to cover the syllabus.

Data revealed that 47.0 per cent of the respondents were dissatisfied with the cooperation of the management.

Majority of the worker teachers (54.5%) expressed satisfaction with the help rendered by the unions in conducting unit level classes. Further analysis of the data on the levels of satisfaction regarding the support given by union and the type of the union revealed that an overwhelming majority (75.0%) of the worker-teachers belonging to the leftist unions expressed dissatisfaction with the union with regard to its workers' education programmes.

It is also found that large number of (47.0%) of the respondents were dissatisfied with the Education Officer's role in conducting unit level classes. They were critical of the attitude of the educational officers.

Perceptions of Worker-Trainees, Management Personnel and Trade Union Officials

The perception of worker-teachers on different aspects of the programme were cross checked with that of the worker-trainees, trade union officials and management personnel.

Reasons for Workers Joining the Programme

A little over 40.0 per cent of the worker-teacher reported that for gaining knowledge the workers undergo training. This view of worker-teachers was corroborated by the perception of the trade unions and worker-trainees (57.9 per cent of the worker-trainees, 44.0 per cent of the trade unions officials) who also found that for gaining knowledge only the workers join the scheme. Contrary to this management personnel reported (53.3%) that study tour is the major attraction, the pursuit of knowledge occupies second position. Dissimilarity of perceptions among the respondents may be attributed to the conflict of interests. Sarma A.M. (1980), and Unnithan (1990) also found that workers join the programme to gain knowledge, while Virmani (1986) found study tour is the main attraction for workers joining the programme.

Regularity of Unit Level Classes

Regularity of unit level classes was also examined and it was found that majority of the worker-teachers reported that unit level classes were regularly conducted while the other three categories of respondents did not share the perception of the worker-teachers. The CBWE claims the implementation of the scheme at all levels (including unit level classes) is quite satisfactory. But these claims are not based on ground realities as the study revealed that the classes are conducted only on paper. This situation contradicts the claims of the worker teachers who claimed that about 60 per cent attendance at the unit level classes.

Duration of Unit Level Classes

Majority of worker-teachers (52.0%) and trainees (69.4%) reported that the duration of the unit level class is not sufficient and needs to be increased. The perceptions of the worker-teachers and trainees are quite contrary to that of management personnel who found the duration a prolonged affair and it needs to be curtailed. And unions were non-committal. Prolonging the duration means loss of man-hours to the industry, hence management does not favour extension of the period.

Study Tour and Time Off

The result of the data on the question whether the level of interest in workers education be sustained without study tour and time-off show that substantial percentage (40.3%) of worker-teachers reported that without study tour and time-off the programme at the third stage cannot be run. This may be the result of their long experience of running unit level classes and interaction with the worker-trainees to the programme as a whole. The worker-trainee refuted the worker-teachers views by claiming that without study tour also the programe can be run. They also told that the course must be designed in such a way that enlivens the interest of the trainee. In tune with the management thinking the respondents from this group expressed the view that the training programme collapses once the study tour and time-off are withdrawn.

Management and Unions

Analysis of the data on the above statement revealed that half of the worker-teachers (49.2%) majority of worker-trainees (57.1%) trade unions officials (52.8%) share the view that management is not interested in workers education, while majority of the management personnel disagreed with this. In the study it has been found that the management respondents consistently exhibited indifferent attitude toward the programme. Rama Swamy (1986) who found that employers have been indifferent to the programme also corroborated this view.

No Follow-up Programmes are Undertaken

Majority of the worker-teachers (57.5%) worker-trainees

(63.8%) trade unions leaders (62.3%) felt that management does not draw any follow-up plans for the worker-teachers. They feel that their duty ends with releasing the workers for worker-teacher training. This also goes to prove that the management is apathetic to the whole programme. The main reason for the nominating workers to the worker-teacher-training is that it is a central government programme and the fear that non-compliance with it may land them in trouble.

Unions are not Interested in Workers Education Programme

It has been found that a large number of worker-teachers (47.0%) felt that unions are indifferent to the programme; the same view was shared by the management personnel who reported (51.2%) indifference of unions to the programme. Unions disagreed with this view while trainees (44.9%) did not choose to comment. Extent of union cooperation is dependent on the ideology and to what extent the workers education serves the interest of the union. This show that unions did not want their brethren to improve their level of knowledge levels, lest, they may pose threat to their leadership. Virmani (1986), Unnithan (1990), Pant S.C. (1973) found that unions are indifferent to the programme.

Selection of the Worker-Teacher

Selection for worker-teacher training is of crucial importance in the programme. The results of data show that a large number (39.6%) of the worker-teachers, three-fourths of the trainees (76.4%) majority of the management personnel (56.7%) and a substantial number of trade unions agreed with the statement that there should be some minimum educational qualification for the worker-teacher training. That majority of respondents endorsed the statement shows that much needs to be done to revamp the selection procedure. Virmani (1986) also favoured some qualifications for the worker-teacher-training programme. Sarma, A.M. (1980) suggested that workers with right aptitude, attitude and abilities should be sponsored for worker-teacher training course.

Syllabus for Unit Level Classes

There are different views on the syllabus. Some opine, it is management oriented, some call it union biased, others feel that it is not relevant. The analysis of the data suggests that none of the parties share the view that it is either anti-management or anti-unions implying that is a balanced one. An overwhelming majority of the worker-teachers (74.3%), majority of the trade union officials (51.0%) and management personnel (51.7%) a large percentage of worker-trainees (46.1%) disagreed with the statement that it is anti-union. Though our data refute the view that it is anti-union, Virmani (1986) commented that management oriented subjects were loaded in the syllabus.

Majority of the respondents in all the four categories also disagreed with the statement that it is anti-management.

The relevance of the syllabus was also probed and the data clearly suggest that the syllabus is not relevant to meet the day to day requirements of the workers. Majority of the worker-teachers (61.2%), worker-trainees (63.8%), substantial percentage of management personnel (43.4%) agreed with the statement that it is not relevant. These views endorse the findings of Virmani (1986) and Rama Swamy (1986) who hold that the syllabus hardly reflects working experiences in the enterprise, and trade union. He found there is no congruence between objectives and syllabus. Hopkins (1968) found the syllabus is too narrow, lack spontaneity, over uniform and stereotyped. According to Sarma (1980) syllabus should be more flexible to suit the needs of different groups. Unions and managements feel it is biased against each other. Sub committee of the regional advisory committee found syllabus was lacking in trade union orientation.

The data on syllabus underpins the need to restructure it, and the routine review of the syllabus by the board hardly meets the purpose. It should be based on the feedback from the workers and the review has to be done in all seriousness.

Education Officer and Targets

Analysis of the data suggest that majority of the worker-teachers (50.7%) management personnel (56.7%) and nearly half of the worker-trainees (48.8%) and a substantial number of trade union officials (39.5%) endorsed the view that E.Os are interested in meeting their targets only. They try to meet the target by hook or crook. In their enthusiasm to meet the target, they play into the hands of the worker-teacher who sometimes manages the show and undermines the very purpose of the unit level classes. Irregularity in conducting the classes, non-conduction of classes are among the criticisms leveled by the workers and the education officer does not seem to pay any heed to these charges.

Workers Education is Promoting Fighting Culture

Majority of the worker-teachers (64.9%) worker-trainees (52.0%) nearly fifty per cent of the trade union officials did not agree to the statement that it is promoting fighting culture. However, it is pertinent to note that a substantial number of management personnel (47.5%) and nearly one-third of the worker-trainees and a significant number of trade unionists, agree with the statement. It suggests that the tone and tenor of workers is becoming strident. This may be due to poor supervision of unit level classes and faulty selection procedures and union rivalry.

Workers Education be made Compulsory

Analysis of the data on the question of making the training under the programme compulsory suggests that except for worker-teachers (an overwhelming majority, 74.0%) none of the parties agreed with the statement. This indicates their opposition to anything that is compulsory and implying that undergoing training is to be left to the choice of the individual worker.

Worker-teacher Should Train Two Batches

Earlier reports of under utilisation of worker-teachers and suggestion of optimum utilisation of worker-teachers prompted the researcher to probe the respondents' views on this issue. The results suggest an overwhelming majority of the worker-teachers (77.0%) favoured the idea that worker-teacher should train two batches. And this view is not shared by others particularly unions (49.1%) management personnel (62.5%). This may be due to the fact that two batches means more unit level classes and loosing of more number of man hours.

Trade Union should Takeover the Function of Education

The results of the data show that majority of the worker-teachers (64.9%), trade unions (51.9%) and a substantial number of trainees did not agree with the statement that trade union should takeover the responsibility of worker education. This is the ultimate goal of the programme. Even after 53 years since its inception, the unions are not yet ready to shoulder the responsibility.

OUTCOME: PERCEPTIONS OF WORKER-TEACHERS, TRAINEES, UNIONS AND MANAGEMENT PERSONNEL

Productivity

The results of the data presented in the preceding pages revealed that majority of the worker-teachers (53.7%); union officials (55.7%) found improvement in the productivity mindedness. While a large group of worker-trainees (46.1%) were non-commital and majority of the management personnel found no improvement in the productivity mindedness perception. Swaraj Bandopadhya (1977), Rizva & Khan (1984) found improvement in the productivity consciousness among workers. Our results endorse their findings. INTUC (1965) found no improvement in productivity.

Rights and Duties

With regard to the awareness about rights and duties, majority of the respondents of all categories were in agreement that there was some improvement in the awareness about rights and duties. Sarma A.M. (1980), Bandopadhya (1977) found improvement in awareness about rights and duties.

Leadership Qualities

With regard to the development of leadership qualities, there has been unanimity among worker-teacher (57.5%); trainees (51.2%) and union officials (64.1%) that there has been some improvement in the leadership qualities while management personnel (45.8%) did not subscribe to this view. Allah Mahar (1981), Devaki Devi (1983), Swaraj Bandopadhya (1977) found improvement in the leadership qualities of worker-teachers. Further enquiries revealed that the majority of worker teachers (58.2%) occupied positions in the industry/union after undergoing training while 20 per cent of the trainees reported ascendancy. A thorough probe into the nature of posts held by the worker-teacher revealed that majority of them (82%) occupied membership positions in the various committees that operate in the industry and around 18.0 per cent of them occupied leadership positions in the union. One of the objectives of the workers education programme is to develop leadership from the rank and file workers, and it is pertinent to note that an insignificant number of workers trained in the unit level classes occupied leadership positions.

Labour-Management Relations

Worker-teachers (64.9%), trainees (60.2%), union officials (54.7%) found improvement in the labour-management relations after training while the management personnel did not share this positive outcome. Swaraj Bandopadhya's (1977) findings corrborated with our findings.

Discipline Consciousness

With regard to discipline consciousness, majority worker-teachers (59.7%) and worker-trainees (71.6%) are in agreement that there is improvement in discipline consciousness while management and unions do not share the same view. Swaraj Bandopadhya (1977) endorsed the findings while Unnithan (1990) found increase in indiscipline among workers after training.

Suggestions

1. *Participation of Women Workers:* The data on the participation of workers in the programme of workers education clearly pointed out that women's participation in the programme is absymally low. Efforts must be made to encourage women to participate in the programme. Separate full time unit level classes of one week duration for women be organised to facilitate their involvement in the programme as the present timings of ULC are not convenient to them. Improved participation of women in the Workers Education Programme will go a long way in achieving the objectives of equality, justice and empowerment of women. ILO is providing financial assistance to the workers education for women with the intention of achieving the above goals. Improved participation of women ensures larger and active participation of women in the workers organisation, access to leadership positions and responsibilities and sponsorship of special trade union services to women workers (Agostinone, V., 1984).

2. *Broad Based Union Participation:* The data on the respondents unions revealed that Centrists Unions are participating and other unions' participation is low. This may be due to the fact that nomination for training programme is vested in the union and the ruling party union is taking advantage of this and nominating their workers in large numbers. Some of the national federations of trade unions are reluctant to be associated with the programme arguing that the thrust of the board is to domesticate workers (Ramaswamy, 1986). The programme must be made broad based and the board should strive to gain wider acceptance among all the federations.

3. *Participation of Non-unionised Members:* As the power of nominating the worker is with the union, non-union members, though attracted by the programme, have lesser chances of undergoing training programme: It is suggested that selection of worker should be entrusted to the committee consisting of management and workers representatives, at the unit level. This committee should look after the entire workers' education function. Selection of workers for worker-teacher training, unit level classes, monitoring and

supervision of the classes, coordinating the activities with the board be entrusted to the committee.

4. *Encouraging White-collared Educated and Young Workers:* The results of the research show that the programmes are not able to attract white-collared, educated and young workers. Efforts must be made to stimulate interest among these sections by making the programmes more attractive, catering to their needs and interests. Participation of educated, white-collared and young workers in the worker-teacher-training programme will improve the quality of teaching in the unit level classes and sustains the programme.

5. *Selection of Worker for Worker-Teacher Training:* The present method of selection *i.e.* union nominating the worker and management releasing him, should be replaced with a joint-decision of management and workers representatives. The committee which has been mentioned earlier be entrusted with the job of selecting the workers for WTT. The committee has to evolve a sound criteria for selecting the worker for the training. Workers with 10+2 qualification and with an aptitute for teaching should form the criteria.

6. *Syllabus: (a)* Data on the syllabus suggest that topics like 'know your country', 'know your industry', 'productivity education', 'trade union movement' were not favoured by the respondents. The time for covering these items be shortened. *(b)* The topic 'communication techniques' was allotted 90 hours and the respondents were not favourably disposed to it. Less emphasis be placed on the theoretical aspects, more efforts be made to provide training them in the practical aspects of communication techniques like teaching practice, use of audio-visual aids. *(c)* Topics which sustain the interest of the workers be included. Inclusion of civil and criminal laws, provident fund, employees insurance, grievance redressal system, Information Technology and disciplinary procedure is suggested. More emphasis be placed to promote the capacity building of the workers, particularly training in globalisation, compatibility skills be provided to them. Review of the syllabus must be taken in all seriousness. Regional workshops involving the academicians, worker-teachers, trainees, trade union representatives, management personnel be conducted to get the feedback. These recommendations are to be discussed

threadbare by the syllabus review committee and the draft syllabus be circulated to all concerned. After finishing these exercises only, the syllabus be given final approval. *(e)* The syllabus should not be uniform for all categories of workers in the unit level classes and it should vary according to the educational and industrial background of the respondents.

Fernau (1983) listed the inclusion of the following subjects in the workers education programme. Education for ageing, health education, continuing professional education, education for civic and social responsibility, education for personal adaptation, education for functional competency and education for teachers of adults. He pleads that education for ageing needs attention as unprecedented number of working people are retiring at an early age due to economic recession. Any type of education to improve competency in coping with problems at work or in life should form part of workers education programme.

Syllabus review committee (1994) suggested the inclusion of the topics like new economic policy, modernisation and surplus labour, retraining and national renewal fund, industrial sickness, achievement motivation, environment and pollution control (p. 11).

7. *Training:* Results of the data on training suggest that it needs overhauling. In the light of the varying responses to the coverage, level of inputs, involvement, training methodology, communication in the training programme it is suggested that separate worker-teacher training programme be offered to the workers based on similar education, job, experience, so as to ensure homogeneity and make the training effective. Homogeneity of the trainees/group facilitates the transfer of knowledge in the training programme, reduces differences in perceptions with regard to its efficacy. The level of communication and the level of inputs and the quality of training material and methodology of training be in tune with the background of the group. Homogeneity of the group affords flexibility in arranging the training modules. *(b)* Considering the poor ratings given to the training methodology by the respondents it is suggested that emphasis on lecture method be reduced and use of participatory training methods, extensive use of audio-visual aids should be given prominence. Selection of teaching

methods should vary according to the composition of the group. All the regional centers should be equipped with the overhead projectors and must be used in the training programme. It has been noticed that the audio-visual aids are not being used even though the centres have been equipped with these instruments. *(d)* Education officers should specialise in some subjects and encourage the involvement of independent, neutral, outside experts, particularly academics from universities and the subjects like labour laws must be handled by legal experts only. *(e)* The regional centres should have atleast one education officer with Bachelors degree in educational technology (B.Ed.). This will facilitate the effective training of workers in the teaching methodologies. *(f)* The present duration of worker-teacher training be reduced and in its place short term training programmes of one week duration be organised at short intervals as they are proved to be effective. Managements have also less difficulty in nominating the workers for short term courses.

Unit Level Classes

Unit level classes evoked criticism as they are far from effective. It is suggested that the present system be dispensed with and in its place full time unit level classes of one week duration be organised by the management itself by roping the service of worker-teacher. The data also suggested that full-time unit level classes were favoured by the respondents. This will also help to reduce the dependency of education officer on worker teacher for achieving the targets of unit level classes. The role of the central board for workers' education should end with training of worker teachers and conducting unit level classes be left to the complete discretion of the management. *(d)* To elicit the cooperation of the management and unions for the programme, the regional advisory committees be made more broad based involving personnel from the labour law enforcement machinery, academics, trade union leaders and management of the private sector and members of the chamber of commerce. The meetings must be conducted regularly and the managements must be urged to cooperate with the board in organising the programme. *(c)* Emphasis on conducting the unit level classes may be reduced and the board should conduct more need based courses of shorter duration. *(d)* The board should make efforts to enroll the candidates from new and uncovered industries in these centres. *(e)* The board should make efforts to develop the regional centres into colleges of labour education and undertake research in the field of workers education and allied matters. A full fledged research wing may be established by the board.

Cooperation of Union and Management

(a) Indifference of unions to the workers education be minimised by eliminating the outsiders from the leadership positions of unions by amending the Trade Unions Act of 1926. Presence of outsiders in the union is likely to hinder the effectiveness of the programme as they feel workers education is a threat to their leadership. *(b)* To make the unions run on sound lines and democratically, it should be stipulated that training in workers education be made a criteria, for eligibility to contest for any post in the union executive and for all the bi-partite committees. This will ensure the cooperation of unions and phasing out of outsiders from the leadership positions.

Objectives of the Scheme

The objectives of the workers education programme be modified and capacity building among workers be given prominence. It is pertinent to note that enhancing the quality and content of workers education programme was one of the items on the agenda of the 36th session of the Indian Labour Conference. ILC recommended that the scope, coverage, dimensions of the workers education be redefined to encompass capacity building of workers.

Education Officers

The status, pay scales of the education officers be improved to encourage them to put more efforts to make them scheme a successful one. The emphasis on targets be reduced, and efforts be made to improve the quality of programme. The practice of Education Officers conducting programmes outside the regional centres be dispensed with as lot of time, money and expertise is wasted.

Infrastructure

Library facilities in the regional centre should be upgraded and quality books of good standard be acquired and be made available to the trainees. The classroom in the regional centres needs to be provided with all facilities (good lighting, ventilation, fans, chairs and tables etc.). Internet facility is to be provided to all the regional centres.

Financing the Programme

Education cess should be imposed on employer to fund the workers' education programme.

Areas of Research

The field of workers education offers many areas for research. Impact studies based on experimental design, studies education officers and their status, working conditions, and problems, working of the trade unions with trained workers, contribution of trained workers in improving the labour-management relations, education and training programme of unions, workers education and voluntary retirement scheme and assessment of the programmes for the unorganised sector. These areas need to be further investigated.

Bibliography

Agostinone, V. (1984), Promoting the Rights of Working Women, *Labour Education*, No. 55, pp. 4-7.

Ajit Mathur (1994), "The Future of Trade Unions", *Indian Journal of Social Work*, LV, No. 2, April.

Anderson Arnold, "Education and Society", *International Encyclopaedia of Social Sciences*, The McMillan Company & The Free Press, New York, Vol. 31, pp. 517-525.

All India Trade Union Congress (1952), Report of the Annual Convention, AITUC, New Delhi.

Anjaneyulu, V. (1981), "Trade Unions and Workers Education for Participative Management", *Indian Labour Journal*, Vol. 22, No. 2, p. 175.

Ashok Pratap Singh (1989), *Industrial Productivity: A Psychological Perspective*, Sage Publications, New Delhi.

Bandopadhyay, Swaraj, I. (1977), *Impact of Workers Education—A Case Study*, Workers Education Central Board for Workers Education, pp. 39-45.

Barbasu, J. (1955), *Universities and Unions in Workers' Education*, Harper & Bro., New York.

Bert F. Hoselitz (1965), "Investment in Education and Its Political Impact in Coleman", James S. (Ed.), *Education and Political Development*, Princeton University Press.

Berteisen (1975), "Adult Education: A Position Paper", unpublished paper submitted to UNESCO.

Bharat Wakhlu (1997), "Effective Approaches for Training and Development", *Personnel Today*, NIPM Publication, Calcutta, April-June, Vol. XVIII, No. 1, pp. 17-21.

Bodete, Thomas (1951), The Right to Education, UNESCO. UNESCO and Its Programme VII.

Bottomore, T.B. (1975), *Sociology: A Guide to Problems and Literature*, Blackie & Son (India) Ltd., Bombay.

Brown, Charles (1989), "Empirical Evidence on Private Training. In Investing in People", Background paper, Vol. I, Washington D.C., Commission on Workforce Quality and Labour Market Efficiency, US Dept. of Labour.

Carter V. Good (Ed.) (1959), *Dictionary of Education*, McGraw Hill Company, New York.

CBWE (1958), *Rules and Regulations of the Central Board for Workers Education*, CBWE, Nagpur.

CBWE (1967), *Report of the Evaluation of Sub-committee of the Local Committee*, Workers Education Centre, May, Bombay.

CBWE (1967), A Report of the Regional Advisory Committee on Workers' Education.

CBWE (1994), *Report of the Syllabus Review Committee on Training Programmes of CBWE*, Nagpur, July, p. 14.

Chansarkar, M.A. (Ed.) (1969), "Impact of Workers Education in Bharat Heavy Electricals Ltd., Hyderabad", A Diagnostic Study WEC, Hyderabad, July.

Chansarkar, M.A. (Ed.) (1969), "Impact of Workers Education in Binod Mills Co. Ltd., Ujjain", A Diagnostic Study, WEC, Indore, July.

Chansarkar, M.A. (Ed.) (1969), "Impact of Workers Education in Calcutta State Transport Corporation, Calcutta: A Diagnostic Study, WEC", Calcutta, June.

Chansarkar, M.A. (Ed.) (1969), "Impact of Workers Education in E.I.D. Parry Ltd., Ranipet", Tamil Nadu, A Diagnostic Study, WEC, Madras, July.

Chansarkar, M.A. (Ed.) (1969), Impact of Workers Education in Government Central Press, Bombay: A Dignostic Study, May.

Chansarkar, M.A. (Ed.) (1969), Impact of Workers Education in the Indian Rare Earths Ltd., Udyogmandal: A Diagnostic Study, WEC, Alwaye, May.

Chansarkar, M.A. (Ed.) (1969), Impact of Workers Education in TISCO Group of Colleries (Dhanbad): A Diagnostic Study, WEC, Dhanbad, September.

Chansarkar, M.A. (Ed.) (1969), *Diagnostic Studies*, CBWE, Nagpur.

Chansarkar, M.A. (Ed.) (1982), Twenty-fourth Annual Report, p. 14.

Cohan, F.M. (1943), *Workers' Education in War and Peace.* Workers' Education Bureau, New York.

Coolie, Verner (1962), A Conceptual Scheme for the Identification and Classification Process for Adult Education, Adult Education Association.

David A. Cecenzo, Stephen P. Robins (1989), *Personnel/Human Resource Management,* Prentice Hall of India, New Delhi.

Dave E. Marcotte (2000), Continuing Education, Job Training and the Growth of Earnings Inequality, *Industrial and Labour Relations Review,* Vol. 53, No. 4, July, p. 621.

Devaki Devi, P. (1983), Worker Teachers lead the Trade Unions: Impact of Workers Education, April, CBWE, Nagpur, pp. 27-30.

Dewey, John (1944), *Democracy and Education,* McMillan Co., New York.

Divensen (1960), Report of the Ninth Annual Convention, Presidential Address, Hon S., pp. 14-15.

Durkheim, Emile (1956), *Education and Society,* The Free Press.

Earl R. Bran Blett (1961), "Maintenance of Discipline", *Management of Personnel Quarterly,* Vol. 1, No. 1, Autumn, p. 10.

Fernau Curt (1983), Workers' Education in the Nineties, *Labour Education,* No. 52, pp. 7-10.

Fernau, C. (1984), What is Workers' Education? An Attempt at Clarification, *Labour Education,* No. 57, pp. 3-4.

Francis Green, Stephen Machin and David Wilkinson (1999), "Trade Unions and Training Practices in British Work Places", *Industrial and Labour Relations Review,* Vol. 52, No. 2, Jan., pp. 179-195.

Ghosh, Subratesh (1960), *Trade Unionism in Underdeveloped Countries,* Calcutta.

Ghosh, B.B. (1954), *Current Problems and Practices in Workers' Education,* ILO, Geneva.

Giri, V.V., *Labour Problems in Indian Industry,* Asia Publishing House, Bombay, pp. 77-80.

Govt. of India (1982), Report of the Syllabus Review Committee on Training Programmes of Central Board of Workers Education, CBWE, Nagpur.

Govt. of India (1969), Report of National Commission on Labour, Ministry of Labour, Employment and Rehabilitation, Chapter-8, Training Industrial and Workers Education, pp. 80-92.

Govt. of India (1971), Recommendations of the Estimates Committee, Fourth Report, Ministry of Labour and Rehabilitation, Workers Education Programme, p. 14.

Govt. of India (1967), "Report of the Committee on Workers Education", *National Commission on Labour,* Delhi, p. 28.

Govt. of India (1982), Workers Participation in Management and Workers Education, *Indian Labour Year Book,* 1980-81, p. 378.

Govt. of India (1956), Second Five Year Plan Report, Planning Commission, Govt. of India Publications, New Delhi.

Govt. of India (1931), Report of the Royal Commission on Labour, New Delhi.

Hamblin (1985), An Introductory Course on Teaching and Training Methods for Management Development, Sterling Publishers, New Delhi.

Harriet Katz (1978), Workers Education or Education for Workers, *Social Service Review,* The University of Chicago Press, Chicago.

Harry Laidler (1973), In William Floyd (Ed) Social Progress (Arbitration) Quoted in *Workers Education in India* by N.K. Kakkar, Sterling Publishers, New Delhi.

Hasley Frazis, Maury Gittleman and Mary Joyce (2000), Correlates of Training: An Analysis using both Employer and Employee Characteristics, *Industrial and Labour Relations Review,* Vol. 53, No. 5, April, pp. 443-462.

Hasley *et. al.* (Ed.) (1961), *Education, Economy and Society,* Free Press, New York.

Henri, Fayol (1951), *General and Industrial Management,* Pitman Publishing Company, New York.

Hind Mazdoor Sabha (1948), *Manifesto of Hind Mazdoor Sabha (HMS),* New Delhi.

Horne, H.H. (1932), *The Democratic Philosophy of Education,* McMillan, New York.

Holmstrom, Mark (1985), *Industry and Inequality: The Social Anthropology of Indian Labour,* Orient Longman, New Delhi.

Hopkins, P.G.H. (1968), *Workers Education in India,* CBWE, Nagpur.

Hurley (1965), Quoted in Cyrel Bibby *The Scientific Humanist, Hurley in the Educated Man* (ed.) Paulorash Andrea, M., Kalamrias, and Henry Y. Perkinsore, Jolible & Sons, pp. 266-267.

INTUC (1965), Labour Policies and Programmes in the Fourth Five Year Plan, Chapter II, New Delhi, INTUC Publication, 49.

Indian Adult Education Association (1958), Workers Education, New Delhi, IAEA.

Indian Adult Education Association (1963), Trade Unions and Workers Education. Report of a Workshop held at the Shafique Memorial from April 24 to 28, p. 36.

ICFTU (1956), *Training the World Unionists*, ICFTU, Brussels.

ICFTU, Education—The Key to Labour Progress, ICFTU (Report of the International Seminar), Brussels, p. 2.

ILO (1976), *Workers' Education and Its Techniques*, Geneva.

ILO (1957), Methods and Techniques of Workers Education, ILO Meeting of Experts on Workers Education, ILO, Geneva.

ILO (1984), India: The Central Board of Workers Education Celebrates Its 25th Birthday (under Labour Education in the World), *Labour Education*, No. 54, ILO Issue, Geneva.

ILO, *An Introductory Course on Teaching and Training Methods for Management Development*, Sterling Publishers (ILO Office), New Delhi.

INTUC (1960), Report of 12th Annual Session, 1959-60.

INTUC (1965), *Labour Policies and Programmes in the Fourth Five Year Plan*, Chapter II, INTUC, Publications, New Delhi.

Jefferson, Thomas (1989), Quoted in *Education and Democracy* by N.V. Sukla, Concept, New Delhi.

John M. Pfiffner (1955), *The Supervision of Personnel Human Relations in the Management of Man*, Prentice Hall Inc., New York, pp. 345-363.

Kakkar, N.K. (1973), *Workers Education in India*, Sterling Publications, New Delhi.

Ketkar, S.V. (1909), *The History of Caste in India*, Ithaca, Tayer and Carpenter.

Kubr, M. (1983), "Principles for Selection of Teaching and Training Methods" in *An Introductory Course in Teaching Methods for Management Development*, ILO Office, Sterling Publishers, New Delhi, 1983, p. 1.

Lendman, Edward (1984), Quoted by Fernau in What is Workers Education: An Attempt at Clarification, *Labour Education*, No. 7, pp. 3-5.

Lewis, Arthur (1962), Education and Economic Development, *International Social Science Journal*, Vol. XIV, p. 688.

Lillard, Lee A., and Hang W. Tan (1996), *Private Sector Training, Who Gets it What are Its Effects?*, California, Rand Corporation.

Livingstone, Richard, *Some Tasks for Education*, Oxford University Press, London.

Lynch, Lisa and Sandra E. Black (1998), "Beyond the Incidence of Employer—Provided Training", *Industrial and Labour Relations Review*, Vol. 52, No. 1, October, pp. 64-81.

Lynch, Lisa M. (1992), "Private Sector Training and the Earnings of Young Workers", *American Economic Review*, Vol. 82, No. 1, pp. 299-312.

Madan, G.R. (1975), *India of Tomorrow*, Allied Publishers, New Delhi.

Madhusudhana Rao, M. (1986), *Labour Management Relations and Trade Unions Leadership: A Behavioural Study of Union Leaders*, Deep & Deep Publications, New Delhi, p. 150.

Mashah Alhah (1986), A critical study of the workers' education schemes in India with special reference to their role in Govt. of India Press (unpublished thesis) in M.B. Buch (ed.), *Third Survey of Research in Education*, New Delhi, National Council of Educational Research and Training, p. 1004.

Marshall Alfred (1961), *Principles of Economics*, ELBS and McMillan & Co. Ltd., London.

Mansbridge, Albred (1903), Quoted in Peffer's *New Schools for Older Students*, McMillan, London, 1926.

Mathur, A.S. and Mathur, J.S., *Trade Union Movement in India*, Chaitanya Publishers, Allahabad.

Mathur, V.S. (1964), Role of Labour Education in Developing Economy, *Bombay Labour Journal*.

Mathew, George (1996), Workers Education in Cannanore Spinning & Weaving Mills, Mahe, *Workers Education*, Sept., pp. 36-49.

Mathur, V.S. (1982), *Workers Education Today*, ICFTU, Asian Regional Organisation, New Delhi, pp. 15-16.

Misra, A.C. (1985), National Seminar on Workers Education in the next decade, New Delhi, 9-11 July, Background papers, CBWE, Nagpur, pp. 2-3.

Mitchels, Robert (1959), *Political Parties*, translated by Eden & Cedar Paul, Dover Publications Inc., New York.

Mohisini, S.R. (1973), Adult and Community Education, Indian Adult Education Association, New Delhi.

Mooney, J.D. (1947), *The Principles of Organisation*, Harper & Row Publishing Inc., New York.

Mukherjee (1985), Workers Education in India—Some Recollections—Workshop on Workers Education in India, Organised by the Administrative Staff College of India, Hyderabad.

Nanda Kumar, P. and Ravi Kumar, S. (1994), "Empirical Study of Membership Participation in Trade Union Activities—An Indian Perspective", *Indian Journal of Industrial Relations,* July, Vol. 30, Delhi, p. 75.

Palekar, S.A. (1973), Problems of Wage Policy for Economic Development (231) quoted in S.C. Pant, *Indian Labour Problems,* Allahabad, Chaitanya Publishing House.

Pant, S.C. (1973), *Indian Labour Problems,* Allahabad, Chaitanya Publishing House.

Peffer, Nathaniel (1920), *New Schools for Older Students,* London, MacMillan Co.

Perlman, S. (1926), Education, *Encyclopaedia of Social Sciences,* Vol. XV.

Peterson, Florence (1951), *American Labour Unions,* Sterling Publishers (P) Ltd., New Delhi.

Plato (1933), *The Republic* (with an English translation by Paul Shorey), Heinemann, New York.

Punekar, S.D. (1958), "Outside Leadership of Trade Unions—A Bombay Survey", *Economic Weekly,* Vol. 10, July, pp. 877-879.

Raj Amarnath (1981), Workers Education: An Appraisal, *Yojana,* 1-15 May, Vol. XXV, No. 8, p. 35.

Ramaswamy, E.A. (1985), What Education do Workers Need? *Economic & Political Weekly,* Vol. 18, No. XI, Feb.

Ramaswamy, E.A. (1986), Towards an Enlightened Workforce, *Business India,* pp. 32-41.

Ramanujam, G. (1975), Report of Review Committee on Workers Education, CBWE, Nagpur, p. 223.

Ramanujam, G. (1981), Workers' Education—New Vistas, CBWE, Nagpur.

Raup, R.B. (1933), In William H. Kilpatrick (ed.), *The Educational Frontier,* Century, New York, 1933, p. 108.

Risely, H.H. (1969), *The People of India,* Orient Books Reprint Corporation, Delhi.

Rizvi, P.H. and Khan, M.A. (1984), UGC Research Project on Impact of Workers Education, *Workers Education,* June, pp. 19-21.

Robert, H.H. (1968), *The Learning Society,* Brittanica Perspectives, Chicago.

Robinson, J.W. (1966), "Book Review of An Historical Examination of the Purposes and Practices of the Educational Programme of the United Automobile Workers of America, 1936-1959 by Thomas E. Linton", *Labour History,* Vol. VII.

Ross, J.S. (1942), *Ground Work Educational Theory,* George G. Harraps Co. Ltd., London.

Roy, Nikhil Ranjan (1967), *Adult Education in India and Abroad,* S. Chand & Co. Ltd., Delhi.

Ruskin (1951), Quoted in *Some Tasks for Education* by Richard Livingstone, Oxford University Press.

Sarje Rao, A., Salunkha, "Emerging Trade Unions Leadership", *Indian Journal of Industrial Relations,* Vol. 29, No. 3, Jan.

Sarma, A.M. (1980), Workers Education Scheme—An Evaluation, *Indian Journal of Social Work,* Vol. XLI, July, No. 2, pp. 123-133.

Saxena, S.B. and Parmar, M.N. (1996), Impact of Workers Education on Industrial Workers, *Workers Education,* Sept. pp. 8-14.

Senart, E. (1930), *Caste in India: The Facts and the System,* Translated by S. Denison Ross, London, Metheum & Co.

Sharma, K.L. (1977), New Introduction by K.L. Sharma in *Review of Caste in India* by J. Murdock, Rawat Publications.

Shukla, P.D. (1971), *Life Long Education,* Orient Longman, New Delhi.

Sidhanta, T.N. (1985), Workers Education: A Trade Union Representative's Viewpoint, *Indian Journal of Adult Education,* May, Vol. 46, No. 5, pp. 14-15.

Siqueira, V. (1994), Industrial Relations: Opportunities in the Mid-Nineties, *Indian Journal of Industrial Relations,* Vol. LV, No. 2, April, pp. 256-260.

Socrates (1963), *The Pocket Book of Quotations,* Cardinal Edition, Henry David of New York.

Sodhi, J.S. (1997), Issues, Trends and Developments in Industrial Relations in India and Other South Asian Countries, *Indian Journal of Industrial Relations,* Vol. 32, No. 4, April, pp. 368-369.

Srinivas, M.N. (1966), *Social Change in Modern India,* Berkeley, University of California Press.

Stephen, Robins (1994), *Essentials of Organisational Behaviour,*

Prentice Hall of India, New Delhi.

Styler, W.E. (1966), *Adult Education in India,* Oxford University Press, London.

Tead & Metcalf (1990), Personnel Administration, quoted in B.P. Singh's *Personnel Management and Industrial Relations,* Damport Roy & Sons, New Delhi.

The Hindu (2000), Report on 36th Session of Indian Labour Conference, April 16, p. 8.

United Nations Educational, Scientific & Cultural Organisation (1952), Seminar on Workers' Education, Chateaula Breviere, Paris.

UNESCO (1951), The Right to Education, UNESCO and Its Programme VII, Paris.

UNESCO (1952), Report of the Seminar on Workers Education, UNESCO, Paris, pp. 3-4.

Unnithan, Sivapalan T.R. (1990), An inquiry into the workers education programme in Kerala with a view to suggest improvements (Unpublished Doctoral Dissertation) submitted to University of Kerala.

Urwick, L. (1955), The Elements of Administration, Harper & Bros., New York quoted in John M. Pfiffner, *The Supervision of Personnel Human Relations in the Management of Man,* Prentice Hall Inc., New York.

Venum, Jonathan (1995), "Sources of Training and Their Impact on Wages", *Industrial and Labour Relations Review,* Vol. 48, pp. 812-26.

. ırmani, B.R. (1986), Evaluation of Workers Education Programme (unpublished report), Administrative Staff College of India, Hyderabad.

Virmani, B.R. (1988), Training Workers for Participation in Management: The Indias Experience, *Indian Journal of Training and Development,* Vol. XVIII, No. 2, March-April, pp. 12-17.

Walter Vrooman (1899), Quoted by Peffer in his Book *New Schools for Older Students.*

Whitehead, A.N. (1929), *The Aims of Education,* The MacMillan Co., New York, p. 13.

Index